PYTHON FOR NETWORK ENGINEERS

Master Python to Automate Networking
Tasks and Enhance Network Operations

THOMPSON CARTER

TABLE OF CONTENTS

Introduction

Python for Network Engineers: Master Python to Automate Networking Tasks and Enhance Network Operations

The modern world relies on networks as its backbone, enabling communication, business operations, and critical services. As networks grow in size and complexity, the traditional methods of managing and maintaining them are becoming increasingly inefficient. Manual configurations, troubleshooting, and performance monitoring cannot keep up with the dynamic demands of today's networks. This is where automation, powered by Python, steps in as a game-changer.

This book, **Python for Network Engineers**, is designed to empower network professionals with the knowledge and tools to automate repetitive tasks, enhance operational efficiency, and address the challenges of modern networking environments. By blending the power of Python with real-world networking scenarios, this book provides a practical roadmap to transition from manual processes to a fully automated and efficient network.

Why Python for Network Engineers?

Python has emerged as the go-to programming language for network automation for several reasons:

1. **Simplicity and Readability**:
   - Python's intuitive syntax makes it accessible even to those with little or no programming experience.

2. **Extensive Libraries**:
   - Libraries like Netmiko, NAPALM, and Paramiko provide pre-built tools to interact with network devices.

3. **Multi-Vendor Support**:
   - Python enables seamless integration with devices from Cisco, Juniper, Arista, and other vendors.

4. **Versatility**:
   - Beyond automation, Python can be used for monitoring, visualization, and creating custom tools tailored to specific needs.

5. **Community Support**:
   - A vibrant community of developers and network engineers ensures continuous development and abundant resources.

What You Will Learn

This book takes a comprehensive approach, guiding you through Python fundamentals, practical automation tasks, and advanced techniques. Key areas of focus include:

1. Python Fundamentals for Networking

- Understanding Python basics: variables, data types, loops, and functions.
- Setting up a Python environment tailored for network automation tasks.
- Introducing essential libraries like Netmiko and NAPALM.

2. Automating Network Operations

- Automating routine tasks like configuration backups, device onboarding, and VLAN assignments.
- Implementing Zero-Touch Provisioning (ZTP) to streamline device deployments.
- Writing Python scripts to interact with multi-vendor environments.

3. Advanced Topics in Network Automation

- Using Python for Software-Defined Networking (SDN) and Network Function Virtualization (NFV).
- Building real-time dashboards for network monitoring with frameworks like Dash and Flask.

- Managing IP address allocations and auditing changes in network configurations.

4. Real-World Applications

- Exploring case studies that demonstrate Python's transformative impact on network operations.
- Developing tailored solutions for network upgrades, performance monitoring, and full automation migrations.

Who This Book Is For

This book is written for:

1. **Network Engineers and Administrators**:
   - Looking to automate repetitive tasks and improve efficiency.
2. **IT Professionals**:
   - Eager to transition into the field of network automation.
3. **Students and Enthusiasts**:
   - Interested in learning Python and its applications in networking.
4. **Organizations**:

o   Aiming to adopt automation for scalability and consistency in network management.

Whether you're new to Python or an experienced coder looking to specialize in network automation, this book provides a structured and practical guide to mastering these skills.

What Sets This Book Apart

1. **Practical, Hands-On Approach**:
   o   The book is packed with real-world examples, scripts, and use cases to ensure you can immediately apply what you learn.
2. **Vendor-Agnostic**:
   o   Covers multi-vendor environments, making the content relevant regardless of your existing network infrastructure.
3. **Focus on Real-World Challenges**:
   o   Tackles common pain points in network operations, such as scaling, troubleshooting, and maintaining consistency.
4. **Comprehensive Coverage**:
   o   Starts with the basics and progresses to advanced topics, ensuring a complete learning experience.

How to Use This Book

1. **Follow the Chapters in Sequence**:
   - Each chapter builds upon the previous one, creating a structured path from foundational knowledge to advanced skills.

2. **Experiment with Scripts**:
   - Test and modify the scripts provided in the book to suit your network environment and challenges.

3. **Apply Learnings to Real-World Scenarios**:
   - Use the case studies as blueprints for solving similar challenges in your organization.

4. **Explore Additional Resources**:
   - Leverage the resources provided in the conclusion to deepen your understanding and stay updated.

The Future of Network Engineering

The demand for network automation skills is on the rise as organizations seek to improve efficiency, scalability, and reliability. Python is at the forefront of this transformation, empowering network engineers to manage complex environments with ease and precision. By mastering Python and its applications in networking, you position yourself at the cutting edge of the industry.

This book is your gateway to unlocking the potential of Python for network automation. Whether you're solving day-to-day challenges or designing advanced systems, the skills you acquire here will equip you to lead in this rapidly evolving field.

Let's begin this journey into the exciting world of Python for network engineering and automation. Your path to becoming a more efficient, effective, and future-ready network professional starts now!

Chapter 1: Why Python for Network Engineers?

Introduction to Python's Role in Network Engineering

In the modern world of network engineering, the demand for automation, efficiency, and scalability has grown exponentially. Networks are becoming more complex, with the introduction of technologies like software-defined networking (SDN), multi-cloud environments, and edge computing. The traditional methods of manual configuration and troubleshooting are no longer viable for managing these environments effectively.

Python has emerged as a **go-to language for network engineers** due to its versatility, simplicity, and powerful ecosystem. Whether you're configuring devices, automating repetitive tasks, or integrating with APIs, Python bridges the gap between manual operations and full scale automation.

Key Areas Where Python Is Transforming Network Engineering:

1. **Device Configuration and Management**: Automate repetitive tasks like configuring routers, switches, or firewalls.

2. **Network Monitoring and Analytics**: Gather real-time data on network performance and visualize it.

3. **Security Automation**: Automate threat detection and response by managing access control lists (ACLs), firewall rules, and intrusion detection logs.

4. **API Integration**: Interact with third-party platforms like cloud services, monitoring tools, and vendor-specific software.

Advantages of Python for Network Automation

Python is uniquely suited to the needs of network engineers, offering benefits that align with the demands of the field:

1. **Simplicity and Readability**:
   - Python's syntax is intuitive and easy to learn, even for those without a software development background.
   - Engineers can write scripts quickly, reducing time to deployment.

2. **Extensive Library Ecosystem**:
   - Libraries like **Netmiko**, **Paramiko**, and **NAPALM** provide tools tailored to network automation.

- General-purpose libraries like **requests** for API interaction and **pandas** for data manipulation enhance Python's capabilities.

3. **Cross-Vendor Support**:
   - Python scripts can communicate with devices from various vendors (Cisco, Juniper, Arista, etc.).
   - Multi-vendor libraries like NAPALM simplify automation in diverse environments.

4. **Integration with Modern Tools**:
   - Python integrates seamlessly with monitoring tools (e.g., Nagios, Grafana), SDN controllers (e.g., OpenDaylight), and cloud platforms (e.g., AWS, Azure).
   - It can be used to manage virtualized environments like VMware or Kubernetes.

5. **Community and Open-Source Resources**:
   - Python has a thriving community of developers and network engineers who contribute to open-source projects, ensuring a continuous flow of tools and solutions.

6. **Scalability**:
   - From small-scale tasks like updating a single device to large-scale operations affecting thousands of devices, Python scales effectively.

Real-World Examples of Python in Network Operations

To understand Python's transformative potential, let's examine a few real-world applications:

1. **Automating Device Configuration**:
   - **Scenario**: A network engineer needs to configure 50 routers with similar settings.
   - **Python Solution**: Using libraries like Netmiko, the engineer can automate SSH sessions to push configurations across all devices.
   - **Benefit**: Saves hours of manual effort and reduces the risk of human error.

   Example Code:

```python
from netmiko import ConnectHandler

device = {
    "device_type": "cisco_ios",
    "host": "192.168.1.1",
    "username": "admin",
    "password": "password",
}

connection = ConnectHandler(**device)
config_commands = ["interface GigabitEthernet0/1", "description Configured by Python"]
```

```
connection.send_config_set(config_commands)
connection.disconnect()
```

2. **Network Monitoring and Alerts**:

   o **Scenario**: Monitoring bandwidth utilization on critical links.

   o **Python Solution**: Using the SNMP library, Python can poll devices and send email alerts when thresholds are exceeded.

   o **Benefit**: Enables proactive network management and minimizes downtime.

Example Code:

python

```python
from pysnmp.hlapi import *

iterator = getCmd(
    SnmpEngine(),
    CommunityData("public"),
    UdpTransportTarget(("192.168.1.1", 161)),
    ContextData(),
    ObjectType(ObjectIdentity("1.3.6.1.2.1.2.2.1.10.1"))  # InOctets
)

for errorIndication, errorStatus, errorIndex, varBinds in iterator:
    if errorIndication:
        print(errorIndication)
```

```
elif errorStatus:
    print(f"{errorStatus.prettyPrint()}")
else:
    for varBind in varBinds:
        print(f"Bandwidth: {varBind.prettyPrint()}")
```

3. **Zero-Touch Provisioning (ZTP)**:
   - ○ **Scenario**: Automatically configure new switches when added to the network.
   - ○ **Python Solution**: Using DHCP options and Python scripts, the switch can be auto-configured during boot.
   - ○ **Benefit**: Eliminates the need for manual intervention during onboarding.

4. **Log Analysis and Security**:
   - ○ **Scenario**: Analyzing firewall logs for suspicious activity.
   - ○ **Python Solution**: Using Python to parse log files and detect anomalies.
   - ○ **Benefit**: Improves incident response time and strengthens security.

Example Code:

python

```
with open("firewall_logs.txt") as logs:
    for line in logs:
```

```
if "unauthorized access" in line:
    print(f"Alert: {line.strip()}")
```

5. **Cloud Network Automation**:

   o **Scenario**: Managing network resources in AWS (e.g., VPCs, subnets, security groups).

   o **Python Solution**: Using the **boto3** library to interact with AWS APIs.

   o **Benefit**: Automates infrastructure provisioning and ensures consistency across environments.

   Example Code:

   python

```python
import boto3

ec2 = boto3.client("ec2")
response = ec2.create_vpc(CidrBlock="10.0.0.0/16")
print(f"Created VPC: {response['Vpc']['VpcId']}")
```

Python is revolutionizing the field of network engineering by simplifying complex tasks, reducing manual effort, and enabling automation at scale. Its readability, extensive libraries, and compatibility with modern networking tools make it an indispensable skill for network engineers.

By the end of this book, you'll not only understand Python but also gain practical experience in applying it to real-world networking challenges. From automating configurations to managing network inventory, this journey will empower you to transform how networks are built, managed, and optimized.

In the next chapter, we'll dive into setting up your Python environment and explore the tools you'll need to begin automating networking tasks. Let's get started!

Chapter 2: Setting Up Your Python Environment

Before diving into Python programming for network engineering, it's crucial to set up an efficient development environment. This chapter will guide you through the installation of Python, essential tools, and libraries tailored for network engineering. By the end of this chapter, you'll have a well-configured environment and a basic Python project structure to begin your automation journey.

Installing Python and Essential Tools

1. Installing Python

Python is available for all major operating systems (Windows, macOS, and Linux). Follow these steps to install Python:

- **Windows**:
    1. Download the latest Python version from python.org.
    2. During installation, check the box **"Add Python to PATH"** to simplify command-line access.
    3. Verify installation by running:

        bash

```
python --version
```

- **macOS/Linux**:

    1. Use the built-in package manager.

        ```bash
        # macOS (Homebrew)
        brew install python3

        # Ubuntu
        sudo apt update
        sudo apt install python3 python3-pip
        ```

    2. Verify installation:

        ```bash
        python3 --version
        ```

2. Installing an Integrated Development Environment (IDE)

Choosing the right IDE can streamline your development process. Here are some popular options:

- **Visual Studio Code (VS Code)**: Lightweight, customizable, and ideal for Python development.
    - Install the **Python extension** from the VS Code Marketplace.
    - Command-line installation:

```bash
```

```bash
brew install --cask visual-studio-code  # macOS
```

- **PyCharm**: A feature-rich IDE designed specifically for Python development.
  - Download the Community (free) or Professional (paid) version from JetBrains.
- **Sublime Text or Atom**: Lightweight editors for smaller projects.

3. Setting Up Virtual Environments

Virtual environments help manage dependencies and isolate project-specific libraries, avoiding conflicts between projects.

- **Creating a Virtual Environment**:

```bash
```

```bash
python -m venv env
```

- **Activating the Virtual Environment**:
  - Windows:

```bash
```

```bash
.\env\Scripts\activate
```

  - macOS/Linux:

bash

source env/bin/activate

- **Deactivating the Virtual Environment**:

bash

deactivate

- **Installing Libraries in the Virtual Environment**:

bash

pip install <library_name>

Key Libraries for Network Engineers

Python's rich ecosystem includes libraries tailored for network engineering tasks. Here are the essential ones:

1. Netmiko

A powerful library for automating SSH connections to network devices.

- **Installation**:

bash

pip install netmiko

- **Features**:
  - ○ Automates device configuration and command execution.
  - ○ Supports multiple vendors, including Cisco, Juniper, and HP.
- **Basic Example**:

python

```python
from netmiko import ConnectHandler

device = {
    "device_type": "cisco_ios",
    "host": "192.168.1.1",
    "username": "admin",
    "password": "password",
}

connection = ConnectHandler(**device)
output = connection.send_command("show ip interface brief")
print(output)
connection.disconnect()
```

2. Paramiko

A Python library for handling SSH and SFTP operations.

- **Installation**:

bash

pip install paramiko

- **Features**:
    - ○ Establishes SSH connections.
    - ○ Transfers files via SFTP.
- **Basic Example**:

python

import paramiko

```
ssh = paramiko.SSHClient()
ssh.set_missing_host_key_policy(paramiko.AutoAddPolicy())
ssh.connect(hostname="192.168.1.1",          username="admin",
password="password")
stdin, stdout, stderr = ssh.exec_command("show ip route")
print(stdout.read().decode())
ssh.close()
```

3. NAPALM

A multi-vendor library for network automation.

- **Installation**:

bash

pip install napalm

- **Features**:
  - Provides a consistent interface for interacting with devices from different vendors.
  - Simplifies tasks like configuration changes and data retrieval.
- **Basic Example**:

```python
python

from napalm import get_network_driver

driver = get_network_driver("ios")
device = driver("192.168.1.1", "admin", "password")
device.open()
facts = device.get_facts()
print(facts)
device.close()
```

Setting Up a Basic Python Project Structure

Organizing your project structure ensures scalability and maintainability as your scripts and dependencies grow.

Recommended Directory Layout

```bash
bash

network_automation_project/
|
```

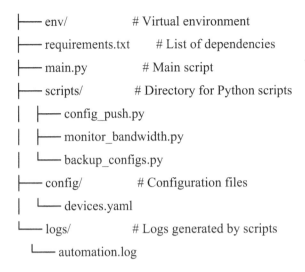

```
├── env/              # Virtual environment
├── requirements.txt   # List of dependencies
├── main.py           # Main script
├── scripts/          # Directory for Python scripts
│   ├── config_push.py
│   ├── monitor_bandwidth.py
│   └── backup_configs.py
├── config/           # Configuration files
│   └── devices.yaml
└── logs/             # Logs generated by scripts
    └── automation.log
```

Steps to Set Up the Structure

1. **Create Folders**:

   bash

   ```bash
   mkdir network_automation_project
   cd network_automation_project
   mkdir scripts config logs
   ```

2. **Initialize Virtual Environment**:

   bash

   ```bash
   python -m venv env
   source env/bin/activate  # Activate the environment
   ```

3. **Create requirements.txt**: Add dependencies for your project:

txt

netmiko
paramiko
napalm
requests

4. **Install Dependencies**:

bash

```
pip install -r requirements.txt
```

5. **Create a Starter Script**: **main.py**:

python

```python
import logging

logging.basicConfig(
    filename="logs/automation.log",
    level=logging.INFO,
    format="%(asctime)s - %(levelname)s - %(message)s",
)

def main():
    logging.info("Starting network automation script...")
    # Add your script logic here

if __name__ == "__main__":
    main()
```

By setting up your Python environment correctly, you lay the groundwork for efficient and organized network automation projects. With Python installed, an IDE configured, and libraries like Netmiko, Paramiko, and NAPALM ready to use, you're equipped to tackle automation tasks with confidence.

In the next chapter, we'll dive into Python basics, ensuring you have a solid understanding of the language's core concepts before applying them to network engineering scenarios. Let's continue building your expertise!

Chapter 3: Python Basics

Before diving into advanced networking tasks, it's essential to master the basics of Python programming. In this chapter, we'll cover the foundational concepts of Python, including variables, data types, control structures, and functions. By the end, you'll write your first Python script tailored for network engineering tasks.

1. Variables and Data Types

Variables

Variables are placeholders for storing data. In Python, you don't need to declare a variable's type explicitly.

Example:

python

```
# Declaring variables
device_name = "Router1"
ip_address = "192.168.1.1"
num_ports = 48

print(f"Device: {device_name}, IP: {ip_address}, Ports: {num_ports}")
```

Data Types

Python supports several data types. Key ones for network engineers include:

- **String (str)**: Text data.

  python

  hostname = "Switch1"

- **Integer (int)**: Whole numbers.

  python

  port_count = 24

- **Float (float)**: Numbers with decimals.

  python

  bandwidth = 100.5

- **Boolean (bool)**: True/False values.

  python

  is_active = True

- **List (list)**: A collection of items.

  python

```
devices = ["Router1", "Switch1", "Firewall1"]
```

- **Dictionary (dict)**: Key-value pairs, useful for storing device details.

python

```
device = {"name": "Router1", "ip": "192.168.1.1", "ports": 48}
```

Example: Working with a Dictionary:

python

```
device = {"name": "Router1", "ip": "192.168.1.1", "ports": 48}
print(f"Device {device['name']} has IP {device['ip']}")
```

---

2. Control Structures

Control structures help manage the flow of your program.

Conditionals

Conditionals allow decision-making based on certain conditions.

Syntax:

python

```
if condition:
    # Code block
elif another_condition:
    # Another code block
```

```
else:
    # Fallback code block
```

Example: Checking Device Status:

python

```
is_active = True

if is_active:
    print("Device is online")
else:
    print("Device is offline")
```

Loops

Loops are used to iterate over sequences or perform repeated actions.

For Loop: Used for iterating over items in a sequence (e.g., lists).

Example: Iterating Over Devices:

python

```
devices = ["Router1", "Switch1", "Firewall1"]

for device in devices:
    print(f"Connecting to {device}")
```

While Loop: Executes as long as a condition is true.

Example: Attempting Connection:

python

```
attempts = 0
while attempts < 3:
    print(f"Attempt {attempts + 1}: Connecting...")
    attempts += 1
```

3. Functions

Functions encapsulate reusable blocks of code, improving maintainability and readability.

Defining a Function
Syntax:

python

```
def function_name(parameters):
    # Code block
    return value
```

Example: Creating a Function to Ping a Device:

python

```
def ping_device(ip):
    print(f"Pinging {ip}...")
    return "Success"

result = ping_device("192.168.1.1")
print(f"Ping result: {result}")
```

Functions with Multiple Parameters

Example: Generate a Device Configuration:

python

```python
def generate_config(device_name, ip_address, ports):
    return f"""
    hostname {device_name}
    ip address {ip_address}
    interface GigabitEthernet0/1
    ports {ports}
    """

config = generate_config("Router1", "192.168.1.1", 48)
print(config)
```

4. Writing Your First Python Script for Network Tasks

Let's apply these concepts to create a simple Python script that fetches and prints device details.

Task: Fetching and Displaying Device Details

We'll create a script to store device information and display it in a formatted output.

Script:

python

```python
# Define a list of devices
devices = [
    {"name": "Router1", "ip": "192.168.1.1", "status": "active"},
    {"name": "Switch1", "ip": "192.168.1.2", "status": "inactive"},
    {"name": "Firewall1", "ip": "192.168.1.3", "status": "active"},
]

# Function to display device details
def display_devices(device_list):
    print("Network Devices:")
    print("-" * 30)
    for device in device_list:
        status = "ONLINE" if device["status"] == "active" else "OFFLINE"
        print(f"Device: {device['name']}, IP: {device['ip']}, Status: {status}")

# Main script logic
if __name__ == "__main__":
    display_devices(devices)
```

Output:

plaintext

Network Devices:

Device: Router1, IP: 192.168.1.1, Status: ONLINE

Device: Switch1, IP: 192.168.1.2, Status: OFFLINE

Device: Firewall1, IP: 192.168.1.3, Status: ONLINE

5. Real-World Application: Automating Ping for Multiple Devices

Let's extend the script to include a ping functionality for each device.

Script:

python

```python
import os

# Define devices
devices = [
    {"name": "Router1", "ip": "192.168.1.1"},
    {"name": "Switch1", "ip": "192.168.1.2"},
    {"name": "Firewall1", "ip": "192.168.1.3"},
]

# Function to ping a device
def ping_device(ip):
    response = os.system(f"ping -c 1 {ip}")
    return response == 0  # True if ping is successful, False otherwise

# Function to check device connectivity
def check_connectivity(device_list):
    for device in device_list:
        success = ping_device(device["ip"])
        status = "ONLINE" if success else "OFFLINE"
        print(f"Device: {device['name']}, IP: {device['ip']}, Status: {status}")

# Main script logic
```

```
if __name__ == "__main__":
    check_connectivity(devices)
```

Output:

plaintext

Device: Router1, IP: 192.168.1.1, Status: ONLINE

Device: Switch1, IP: 192.168.1.2, Status: OFFLINE

Device: Firewall1, IP: 192.168.1.3, Status: ONLINE

This chapter provided an overview of Python's basics, including variables, data types, control structures, and functions. By applying these concepts, you've written your first Python scripts for network tasks, showcasing how Python simplifies common operations like fetching device details and checking connectivity.

In the next chapter, we'll explore **file handling and data parsing**, crucial skills for reading and processing network configuration files and logs. Let's continue building your Python expertise!

Chapter 4: File Handling and Data Parsing

In network engineering, managing configuration files and analyzing data from various formats is a routine task. Python's robust file handling capabilities, combined with its ability to parse text, JSON, and XML, make it an invaluable tool for network automation. This chapter explores how to read, write, and parse different file formats, culminating in a real-world example: parsing router configurations.

---

1. Reading and Writing Configuration Files

Reading Files

Python's built-in functions allow you to open and read files easily.

Example: Reading a Configuration File:

python

```
# Open and read a file
with open("router_config.txt", "r") as file:
    content = file.read()
    print(content)
```

Output:

plaintext

hostname Router1
interface GigabitEthernet0/1
 ip address 192.168.1.1 255.255.255.0
 no shutdown

Writing Files

You can write configuration changes or logs to a file.

Example: Writing to a File:

python

```
config = """
hostname Router2
interface GigabitEthernet0/2
 ip address 192.168.1.2 255.255.255.0
 no shutdown
"""
```

```
with open("new_config.txt", "w") as file:
    file.write(config)
```

Creates a file new_config.txt with the above content.

Appending Data to Files

To append data without overwriting existing content:

Example:

python

```
with open("log.txt", "a") as file:
    file.write("Device Router1 configuration updated.\n")
```

---

2. Parsing Network Data in Different Formats

Parsing Text Files

Text files are common in network operations, often used to store device configurations or logs. Parsing involves extracting meaningful data from such files.

Example: Parsing a Configuration File:

python

```
# Sample configuration file content
config_lines = """
hostname Router1
interface GigabitEthernet0/1
 ip address 192.168.1.1 255.255.255.0
 no shutdown
"""

# Extracting interface information
for line in config_lines.splitlines():
    if "interface" in line or "ip address" in line:
```

```
    print(line.strip())
```

Output:

plaintext

interface GigabitEthernet0/1
ip address 192.168.1.1 255.255.255.0

Parsing JSON Data

JSON is a widely used format for APIs and structured data.

Example: Parsing JSON:

python

```python
import json

# Sample JSON data
json_data = '''
{
    "devices": [
        {"name": "Router1", "ip": "192.168.1.1", "status": "active"},
        {"name": "Switch1", "ip": "192.168.1.2", "status": "inactive"}
    ]
}
'''

# Parse JSON into a Python dictionary
data = json.loads(json_data)
```

```python
# Accessing specific data
for device in data["devices"]:
    print(f"Device: {device['name']}, IP: {device['ip']}, Status: {device['status']}")
```

Output:

plaintext

Device: Router1, IP: 192.168.1.1, Status: active
Device: Switch1, IP: 192.168.1.2, Status: inactive

Parsing XML Data

XML is commonly used in network management systems.

Example: Parsing XML:

python

```python
import xml.etree.ElementTree as ET

# Sample XML data
xml_data = """
<network>
    <device>
        <name>Router1</name>
        <ip>192.168.1.1</ip>
    </device>
    <device>
        <name>Switch1</name>
        <ip>192.168.1.2</ip>
    </device>
```

```
</network>
"""

# Parse XML data
root = ET.fromstring(xml_data)

# Accessing elements
for device in root.findall("device"):
    name = device.find("name").text
    ip = device.find("ip").text
    print(f"Device: {name}, IP: {ip}")
```

Output:

plaintext

```
Device: Router1, IP: 192.168.1.1
Device: Switch1, IP: 192.168.1.2
```

3. Real-World Example: Parsing Router Configurations

Scenario

You receive a configuration file for a router, and your task is to extract specific information like the hostname, interface names, and IP addresses.

Sample Configuration File (router_config.txt):

plaintext

```
hostname Router1
```

```
interface GigabitEthernet0/1
 ip address 192.168.1.1 255.255.255.0
 no shutdown
interface GigabitEthernet0/2
 ip address 192.168.2.1 255.255.255.0
 shutdown
```

Script to Parse the Configuration File:

python

```python
# Function to parse the configuration file
def parse_router_config(file_path):
    with open(file_path, "r") as file:
        config_lines = file.readlines()

    config_data = {
        "hostname": None,
        "interfaces": []
    }

    current_interface = None

    for line in config_lines:
        line = line.strip()
        if line.startswith("hostname"):
            config_data["hostname"] = line.split()[1]
        elif line.startswith("interface"):
            current_interface = {"name": line.split()[1], "ip_address": None, "status":
"shutdown"}
            config_data["interfaces"].append(current_interface)
        elif "ip address" in line:
```

```
        current_interface["ip_address"] = line.split()[2]
    elif "no shutdown" in line:
        current_interface["status"] = "up"


    return config_data


# Parse the file and print results
config = parse_router_config("router_config.txt")


print(f"Hostname: {config['hostname']}")
for interface in config["interfaces"]:
    print(f"Interface: {interface['name']}, IP: {interface['ip_address']}, Status: {interface['status']}")
```

Output:

plaintext

Hostname: Router1
Interface: GigabitEthernet0/1, IP: 192.168.1.1, Status: up
Interface: GigabitEthernet0/2, IP: 192.168.2.1, Status: shutdown

---

Best Practices for File Handling and Parsing

1. **Use Context Managers**:
   o Always use with open() to ensure files are properly closed.

2. **Handle Errors Gracefully**:

○ Use try and except blocks to handle errors like file not found or permission issues.

Example:

python

```
try:
    with open("missing_file.txt", "r") as file:
        content = file.read()
except FileNotFoundError:
    print("Error: File not found.")
```

3. **Validate Data**:

   ○ Ensure the data format (text, JSON, or XML) is as expected before parsing.

4. **Document Parsing Logic**:

   ○ Add comments to explain parsing logic, especially for complex formats.

File handling and data parsing are fundamental skills for network engineers using Python. In this chapter, you learned how to read, write, and parse text, JSON, and XML data, culminating in a real-world example of extracting meaningful information from a router configuration file. These techniques will serve as the foundation for more advanced automation tasks.

In the next chapter, we'll explore **working with APIs**, enabling you to interact with network management tools and cloud platforms programmatically. Let's continue building your Python expertise!

Chapter 5: Working with APIs

Modern network engineering relies heavily on programmatic access to devices, services, and tools, and **REST APIs** (Representational State Transfer Application Programming Interfaces) have become the standard for this interaction. This chapter will explore REST APIs, their importance in networking, and how to use Python's **requests** library to interact with them. We will also provide a real-world example of fetching data from a network monitoring tool's API.

1. Understanding REST APIs and Their Importance in Networking

What Are REST APIs?

A REST API is an architectural style that allows two systems to communicate over HTTP using standard methods like GET, POST, PUT, and DELETE.

Key Features of REST APIs:

- **Stateless**: Each API call is independent and contains all the information needed to process the request.

- **Resource-Oriented**: APIs expose resources (e.g., devices, configurations) that can be accessed or manipulated.
- **Standardized Methods**:
  - **GET**: Retrieve data from the server.
  - **POST**: Create a new resource on the server.
  - **PUT**: Update an existing resource.
  - **DELETE**: Remove a resource.

Why Are REST APIs Important for Networking?

1. **Programmatic Access to Devices and Tools**:
   - APIs provide a way to interact with devices and services programmatically without relying on manual configurations.
2. **Automation and Scalability**:
   - Automate repetitive tasks like device provisioning, monitoring, and configuration updates.
3. **Integration with Third-Party Services**:
   - Network engineers can integrate tools like monitoring platforms (e.g., SolarWinds, Nagios) or cloud services (e.g., AWS, Azure).
4. **Vendor-Agnostic Operations**:
   - REST APIs offer consistent interfaces across different vendors, reducing complexity in multi-vendor environments.

2. Using Python to Interact with APIs

Python's **requests** library simplifies working with REST APIs.

Installing the requests Library
If not already installed:

bash

```
pip install requests
```

Making a Basic API Call
Example: Sending a GET Request:

python

```
import requests

# Sample API endpoint
url = "https://jsonplaceholder.typicode.com/posts/1"

# Send a GET request
response = requests.get(url)

# Print response
print(response.status_code)  # HTTP status code
print(response.json())      # JSON response body
```

Output:

plaintext

200

{'userId': 1, 'id': 1, 'title': 'Sample Title', 'body': 'Sample Content'}

Handling Query Parameters

Many APIs require query parameters for filtering or searching data.

Example: Adding Query Parameters:

python

```
url = "https://jsonplaceholder.typicode.com/posts"
params = {"userId": 1}

response = requests.get(url, params=params)
print(response.json())
```

Output:

plaintext

```
[
  {'userId': 1, 'id': 1, 'title': 'Sample Title', 'body': 'Sample Content'},
  ...
]
```

Authenticating with APIs

APIs often require authentication using tokens or credentials.

Example: Using an API Token:

python

```
url = "https://api.example.com/devices"
headers = {"Authorization": "Bearer YOUR_API_TOKEN"}

response = requests.get(url, headers=headers)
print(response.json())
```

Making a POST Request

Use POST to create new resources.

Example: Creating a New Resource:

python

```
url = "https://jsonplaceholder.typicode.com/posts"
data = {"title": "New Post", "body": "This is a new post", "userId": 1}

response = requests.post(url, json=data)
print(response.status_code)
print(response.json())
```

Output:

plaintext

```
201
{'id': 101, 'title': 'New Post', 'body': 'This is a new post', 'userId': 1}
```

3. Real-World Example: Fetching Data from a Network Monitoring Tool's API

Scenario

You want to fetch network device status information from a monitoring tool's REST API and display the results in a readable format.

API Endpoint Details

- **Base URL**: https://api.network-monitoring-tool.com/devices
- **Authentication**: Bearer token
- **Endpoint**: /devices
- **Method**: GET
- **Response Format**: JSON

Python Script
Step 1: Fetch Device Data

python

```
import requests

# Define the API URL and token
base_url = "https://api.network-monitoring-tool.com"
endpoint = "/devices"
url = f"{base_url}{endpoint}"
```

```python
headers = {"Authorization": "Bearer YOUR_API_TOKEN"}

# Send a GET request to fetch device data
response = requests.get(url, headers=headers)

if response.status_code == 200:
    devices = response.json()
    print("Devices fetched successfully.")
else:
    print(f"Failed to fetch devices: {response.status_code}")
```

Step 2: Process and Display the Data

python

```python
# Display device information
def display_devices(devices):
    print("Device Status Report")
    print("-" * 40)
    for device in devices:
        print(f"Name: {device['name']}")
        print(f"IP Address: {device['ip']}")
        print(f"Status: {device['status']}")
        print("-" * 40)

if response.status_code == 200:
    display_devices(devices)
```

Sample Response from the API

json

```
[
    {"name": "Router1", "ip": "192.168.1.1", "status": "active"},
    {"name": "Switch1", "ip": "192.168.1.2", "status": "inactive"},
    {"name": "Firewall1", "ip": "192.168.1.3", "status": "active"}
]
```

Output:

plaintext

Device Status Report

Name: Router1

IP Address: 192.168.1.1

Status: active

Name: Switch1

IP Address: 192.168.1.2

Status: inactive

Name: Firewall1

IP Address: 192.168.1.3

Status: active

Best Practices for Working with APIs

1. **Read API Documentation**:
   - Understand the required endpoints, parameters, and authentication methods.

2. **Handle Errors Gracefully**:
   - Check HTTP response codes (e.g., 200 OK, 404 Not Found) and handle failures appropriately.

Example:

python

```
if response.status_code != 200:
    print(f"Error: {response.status_code}")
```

3. **Secure API Keys**:
   - Store sensitive information like API keys in environment variables or configuration files.

Example:

python

```
import os
API_TOKEN = os.getenv("API_TOKEN")
```

4. **Use Pagination**:
   - Handle large data sets by implementing pagination if supported by the API.

Example:

python

```
params = {"page": 1}
response = requests.get(url, headers=headers, params=params)
```

5. **Test API Calls**:
   o Use tools like **Postman** or **curl** to test endpoints before implementing them in Python.

APIs are a powerful tool for network engineers, enabling automation and integration with various services and devices. In this chapter, you learned about REST APIs, how to use Python's requests library to interact with them, and implemented a practical example of fetching device data from a network monitoring tool's API.

In the next chapter, we'll explore **networking essentials** and how Python can help automate fundamental networking tasks. Let's continue building your Python skills for network engineering!

Chapter 6: Networking Essentials for Python Developers

Networking is the backbone of modern technology, and understanding its principles is essential for Python developers working in this domain. This chapter provides a comprehensive overview of networking concepts, introduces key protocols, and demonstrates how Python can be applied to automate and enhance networking tasks.

1. Overview of Networking Concepts

OSI Model

The **OSI (Open Systems Interconnection)** model is a conceptual framework that standardizes how different networking devices communicate.

7 Layers of the OSI Model:

1. **Application Layer**: Interfaces with software (e.g., HTTP, FTP, DNS).
2. **Presentation Layer**: Formats data for applications (e.g., encryption, compression).

3. **Session Layer**: Manages connections and sessions.

4. **Transport Layer**: Ensures reliable data delivery (e.g., TCP, UDP).

5. **Network Layer**: Routes packets (e.g., IP).

6. **Data Link Layer**: Handles data transfer between devices on the same network.

7. **Physical Layer**: Transmits raw data over physical media (e.g., cables, Wi-Fi).

Python Application:

- Python operates primarily at the Application and Transport layers, using libraries to interact with protocols like HTTP, SSH, and SNMP.

IP Addresses and Subnetting

- **IP Address**: A unique identifier for devices on a network.
    - IPv4: 192.168.1.1 (32-bit).
    - IPv6: 2001:0db8:85a3:0000:0000:8a2e:0370:7334 (128-bit).
- **Subnetting**:
    - Divides a network into smaller sub-networks.
    - **Example**: A /24 subnet mask allows 256 addresses (e.g., 192.168.1.0/24).

Python Application:

- Python can calculate subnet masks and verify IP ranges using libraries like ipaddress.

Example:

python

import ipaddress

# Validate an IP address
ip = ipaddress.ip_address("192.168.1.1")
print(f"IP Address: {ip}, Valid: {ip.is_private}")

# Create a subnet
subnet = ipaddress.ip_network("192.168.1.0/24")
print(f"Total Addresses: {subnet.num_addresses}")

Routing

Routing directs data packets between networks.

- **Static Routing**: Manually configured paths.
- **Dynamic Routing**: Automated routing using protocols like OSPF, BGP.

Python Application:

- Automate routing configurations via libraries like Netmiko.

2. Understanding Network Protocols

TCP/IP

The **TCP/IP** protocol suite is the foundation of the internet.

- **TCP (Transmission Control Protocol)**:
    o Ensures reliable data transmission.
    o Connection-oriented.
    o Example: File transfer, email.
- **UDP (User Datagram Protocol)**:
    o Faster but unreliable (no error checking).
    o Connectionless.
    o Example: Streaming, DNS queries.

Python Application:

- Use Python's socket library to build TCP/UDP client-server applications.

Example: TCP Client:

python

import socket

# Create a TCP client
client = socket.socket(socket.AF_INET, socket.SOCK_STREAM)

```
client.connect(("www.google.com", 80))
client.sendall(b"GET / HTTP/1.1\r\nHost: www.google.com\r\n\r\n")
response = client.recv(4096)
print(response.decode())
client.close()
```

HTTP

HTTP (HyperText Transfer Protocol) is the protocol for web communication.

- **HTTP Methods**:
    - GET: Retrieve data.
    - POST: Send data.
    - PUT: Update data.
    - DELETE: Remove data.

Python Application:

- Python's requests library simplifies HTTP communication.

Example:

python

```
import requests

response = requests.get("https://api.example.com/data")
print(response.status_code)
print(response.json())
```

SSH

SSH (Secure Shell) is used for secure remote access and command execution.

Python Application:

- Libraries like Paramiko and Netmiko enable SSH automation.

Example:

python

```
from netmiko import ConnectHandler

device = {
    "device_type": "cisco_ios",
    "host": "192.168.1.1",
    "username": "admin",
    "password": "password",
}

connection = ConnectHandler(**device)
output = connection.send_command("show ip interface brief")
print(output)
connection.disconnect()
```

SNMP

SNMP (Simple Network Management Protocol) monitors and manages network devices.

- **MIB (Management Information Base)**: Defines device attributes.
- **OID (Object Identifier)**: Identifies specific data (e.g., bandwidth usage).

Python Application:

- Use the pysnmp library to fetch SNMP data.

Example:

python

```
from pysnmp.hlapi import *

iterator = getCmd(
    SnmpEngine(),
    CommunityData("public"),
    UdpTransportTarget(("192.168.1.1", 161)),
    ContextData(),
    ObjectType(ObjectIdentity("1.3.6.1.2.1.2.2.1.10.1"))  # InOctets
)

for errorIndication, errorStatus, errorIndex, varBinds in iterator:
    if errorIndication:
        print(errorIndication)
    elif errorStatus:
```

```
    print(f"{errorStatus.prettyPrint()}")
else:
    for varBind in varBinds:
        print(f"SNMP Data: {varBind.prettyPrint()}")
```

3. Mapping Python Capabilities to Networking Tasks

Python provides libraries and tools that align with various networking tasks:

Networking Task	Python Tools	Example
IP Validation and Subnetting	ipaddress	Validate IP addresses, calculate subnets.
Device Configuration	Netmiko, Paramiko	Automate CLI commands over SSH.
Monitoring and Alerts	pysnmp, requests	Fetch SNMP data, query monitoring APIs.
Log Analysis	Standard File I/O, re	Parse and analyze log files.
Packet Inspection	scapy	Analyze network traffic and packets.

Networking Task	Python Tools	Example
API Integration	requests, json, xml.etree	Query REST APIs for configuration and monitoring.
Secure File Transfer	Paramiko, ftplib	Automate SFTP and FTP transfers.
Network Simulations	GNS3, Cisco DevNet SDK	Automate simulations using virtual environments like GNS3 or VIRL.

Real-World Example: Automating Network Monitoring

Scenario:

Fetch interface bandwidth utilization using SNMP.

Python Script:

```python
python

from pysnmp.hlapi import *

def fetch_bandwidth(ip, oid):
    iterator = getCmd(
        SnmpEngine(),
        CommunityData("public"),
```

```
        UdpTransportTarget((ip, 161)),
        ContextData(),
        ObjectType(ObjectIdentity(oid))
    )
    for errorIndication, errorStatus, errorIndex, varBinds in iterator:
        if errorIndication:
            print(f"Error: {errorIndication}")
            return None
        elif errorStatus:
            print(f"Error: {errorStatus.prettyPrint()}")
            return None
        else:
            for varBind in varBinds:
                return varBind.prettyPrint().split("=")[1].strip()


# Fetch InOctets for interface 1
ip_address = "192.168.1.1"
oid = "1.3.6.1.2.1.2.2.1.10.1"
bandwidth = fetch_bandwidth(ip_address, oid)
if bandwidth:
    print(f"Bandwidth (InOctets): {bandwidth}")
```

Output:

plaintext

Bandwidth (InOctets): 12345678

This chapter provided a foundational understanding of networking concepts and protocols, highlighting how Python maps to real-world networking tasks. From IP validation to automating SSH commands and fetching SNMP data, Python simplifies and enhances network operations.

In the next chapter, we'll explore **Python and Networking Basics**, diving into sockets, client-server models, and creating Python scripts to interact with networks programmatically. Let's continue mastering Python for networking!

Chapter 7: Python and Networking Basics

Networking forms the backbone of communication in modern computing, and Python provides powerful tools for network programming. In this chapter, you'll learn how to work with Python's socket library to create client-server applications. We'll cover the basics of sockets and build a simple TCP client-server script as a practical example.

1. Introduction to Sockets

What Are Sockets?
A **socket** is an endpoint for sending or receiving data across a network. It serves as a bridge between applications, enabling them to communicate.

Types of Sockets

1. **Stream Sockets (TCP)**:
   - Reliable, connection-oriented communication.
   - Used for applications like HTTP, SSH, and email.
2. **Datagram Sockets (UDP)**:

- o   Fast, connectionless communication.
- o   Used for applications like DNS and video streaming.

Python's socket Library

Python's socket module provides functions for network communication, supporting both TCP and UDP sockets.

Key Methods:

- socket(): Creates a socket.
- bind(): Binds the socket to an address and port.
- listen(): Enables the server to accept incoming connections.
- accept(): Accepts a connection from a client.
- connect(): Connects to a server.
- send() / sendall(): Sends data over the connection.
- recv(): Receives data from the connection.
- close(): Closes the socket.

2. Creating a TCP Client-Server Application

In a typical client-server model:

- The **server** listens for incoming requests.
- The **client** connects to the server and exchanges data.

Step 1: Build the TCP Server
Server Code:

python

```python
import socket

def start_server(host, port):
    # Create a TCP socket
    server_socket = socket.socket(socket.AF_INET, socket.SOCK_STREAM)

    # Bind the socket to the address and port
    server_socket.bind((host, port))

    # Start listening for connections (up to 5 clients)
    server_socket.listen(5)
    print(f"Server listening on {host}:{port}")

    while True:
        # Accept a connection
        client_socket, client_address = server_socket.accept()
        print(f"Connection established with {client_address}")

        # Receive data from the client
        data = client_socket.recv(1024).decode("utf-8")
        print(f"Received from client: {data}")

        # Send a response
        client_socket.send("Message received!".encode("utf-8"))
```

```python
        # Close the client connection
        client_socket.close()

# Start the server
if __name__ == "__main__":
    start_server("127.0.0.1", 8080)
```

Explanation:

1. A TCP socket is created and bound to the specified host and port.
2. The server listens for incoming connections and accepts them.
3. Data is received from the client and a response is sent back.

Step 2: Build the TCP Client
Client Code:

python

```python
import socket

def start_client(host, port, message):
    # Create a TCP socket
    client_socket = socket.socket(socket.AF_INET, socket.SOCK_STREAM)

    # Connect to the server
    client_socket.connect((host, port))
    print(f"Connected to server at {host}:{port}")
```

```
# Send a message to the server
client_socket.send(message.encode("utf-8"))

# Receive a response from the server
response = client_socket.recv(1024).decode("utf-8")
print(f"Server response: {response}")

# Close the connection
client_socket.close()

# Start the client
if __name__ == "__main__":
    start_client("127.0.0.1", 8080, "Hello, Server!")
```

Explanation:

1. The client socket connects to the server.
2. A message is sent to the server, and a response is received.

---

3. Running the TCP Application

1. **Start the Server**:
   - Run the server script to start listening for connections.

   bash

   python server.py

   Output:

plaintext

Server listening on 127.0.0.1:8080

2. **Run the Client**:

   o   Run the client script to connect to the server and send a message.

bash

python client.py

Output:

plaintext

Connected to server at 127.0.0.1:8080
Server response: Message received!

3. **Server Output**:

plaintext

Connection established with ('127.0.0.1', 53512)
Received from client: Hello, Server!

4. Enhancements and Use Cases

Enhancement: Handling Multiple Clients

To handle multiple clients, use threading or asynchronous programming.

Example: Multi-Client Server:

python

```python
import socket
import threading

def handle_client(client_socket, client_address):
    print(f"Connection established with {client_address}")
    data = client_socket.recv(1024).decode("utf-8")
    print(f"Received from client: {data}")
    client_socket.send("Message received!".encode("utf-8"))
    client_socket.close()

def start_server(host, port):
    server_socket = socket.socket(socket.AF_INET, socket.SOCK_STREAM)
    server_socket.bind((host, port))
    server_socket.listen(5)
    print(f"Server listening on {host}:{port}")

    while True:
        client_socket, client_address = server_socket.accept()
        thread = threading.Thread(target=handle_client, args=(client_socket, client_address))
        thread.start()

if __name__ == "__main__":
    start_server("127.0.0.1", 8080)
```

Use Cases for TCP Sockets in Networking

1. **Device Monitoring**:
   - Create a server to listen for status updates from network devices.
   - The client (device) sends periodic health reports.
2. **Configuration Management**:
   - Push configurations to devices using a client-server model.
   - The server stores configurations, and clients retrieve them.
3. **Data Collection**:
   - Collect logs or performance metrics from network devices in real-time.

Best Practices for Network Programming

1. **Use Non-Blocking or Asynchronous Sockets**:
   - For high-performance applications, use libraries like asyncio.
2. **Validate Input**:
   - Sanitize and validate data received from clients to prevent security vulnerabilities.

3. **Handle Exceptions Gracefully**:

    o   Catch errors like connection failures to avoid crashes.

Example:

python

```
try:
    client_socket.connect((host, port))
except socket.error as e:
    print(f"Connection error: {e}")
```

4. **Secure Connections**:

    o   Use ssl to encrypt data for sensitive communications.

5. **Test with Different Environments**:

    o   Test applications in networks with varying latency and bandwidth conditions.

This chapter introduced the fundamentals of Python's socket library and demonstrated how to build a basic TCP client-server application. Sockets are a powerful tool for network communication and can be extended to handle complex use cases like monitoring, data collection, and configuration management.

In the next chapter, we'll explore **automating device configuration with Python**, focusing on using libraries like Netmiko and Paramiko to interact with network devices programmatically. Let's continue automating the network!

Chapter 8: Automating Device Configuration with Python

Automating the configuration of routers and switches is one of the most impactful use cases for Python in network engineering. By leveraging SSH libraries like **Paramiko** and **Netmiko**, you can programmatically interact with network devices, saving time and reducing errors. In this chapter, we'll introduce these libraries, demonstrate how to automate login and configuration, and provide a real-world example of pushing configuration changes across multiple devices.

1. Introduction to SSH Libraries

Paramiko

Paramiko is a Python library for SSH connections and SFTP file transfers. It allows direct communication with network devices using command-line interfaces.

- **Key Features**:
    - SSH session management.
    - Secure file transfers via SFTP.
    - Execution of CLI commands.

- **Installation**:

  bash

  pip install paramiko

Netmiko

Netmiko is built on top of Paramiko and simplifies interactions with network devices by abstracting vendor-specific complexities. It supports multiple vendors, such as Cisco, Juniper, Arista, and more.

- **Key Features**:
  - ○ Vendor-specific command execution.
  - ○ Simplified configuration pushes.
  - ○ Built-in error handling for network automation.
- **Installation**:

  bash

  pip install netmiko

---

2. Automating Login and Configuration

Using Paramiko

Paramiko requires you to manually handle command execution, making it flexible but more complex than Netmiko.

Example: Automating Login with Paramiko:

python

```python
import paramiko

def execute_command(host, username, password, command):
    try:
        # Create an SSH client
        ssh = paramiko.SSHClient()
        ssh.set_missing_host_key_policy(paramiko.AutoAddPolicy())

        # Connect to the device
        ssh.connect(hostname=host, username=username, password=password)

        # Execute the command
        stdin, stdout, stderr = ssh.exec_command(command)
        output = stdout.read().decode()
        print(f"Output from {host}:\n{output}")

        # Close the connection
        ssh.close()

    except Exception as e:
        print(f"Error connecting to {host}: {e}")

# Example usage
execute_command("192.168.1.1", "admin", "password", "show ip interface brief")
```

Using Netmiko

Netmiko simplifies SSH interactions by providing pre-built methods for common tasks.

Example: Automating Login with Netmiko:

python

```
from netmiko import ConnectHandler

def fetch_device_output(host, username, password, command):
    # Define device details
    device = {
        "device_type": "cisco_ios",  # Adjust based on vendor
        "host": host,
        "username": username,
        "password": password,
    }

    try:
        # Establish an SSH connection
        connection = ConnectHandler(**device)

        # Execute the command
        output = connection.send_command(command)
        print(f"Output from {host}:\n{output}")

        # Disconnect
        connection.disconnect()

    except Exception as e:
        print(f"Error connecting to {host}: {e}")
```

```
# Example usage
fetch_device_output("192.168.1.1", "admin", "password", "show ip interface brief")
```

---

3. Real-World Example: Pushing Configuration Changes Across Devices

Scenario

You are tasked with configuring multiple routers with identical settings, such as VLAN assignments and interface descriptions. This would take hours manually but can be automated in minutes with Python.

Step 1: Define the Configuration

Create a list of commands to push to the devices.

python

```python
commands = [
    "interface GigabitEthernet0/1",
    "description Configured by Python Script",
    "ip address 192.168.100.1 255.255.255.0",
    "no shutdown",
    "exit",
    "vlan 100",
    "name Automation_VLAN",
```

]

Step 2: Create the Python Script

Use Netmiko to connect to each device and push the configuration commands.

python

```
from netmiko import ConnectHandler

def configure_devices(devices, commands):
    for device in devices:
        try:
            print(f"Connecting to {device['host']}...")
            connection = ConnectHandler(**device)

            # Push configuration commands
            output = connection.send_config_set(commands)
            print(f"Configuration pushed to {device['host']}:\n{output}")

            # Save configuration
            connection.send_command("write memory")
            print(f"Configuration saved on {device['host']}.")

            # Disconnect
            connection.disconnect()

        except Exception as e:
            print(f"Error configuring {device['host']}: {e}")
```

```
# Define the devices
devices = [
    {"device_type": "cisco_ios", "host": "192.168.1.1", "username": "admin",
"password": "password"},
    {"device_type": "cisco_ios", "host": "192.168.1.2", "username": "admin",
"password": "password"},
]

# Define the commands
commands = [
    "interface GigabitEthernet0/1",
    "description Configured by Python Script",
    "ip address 192.168.100.1 255.255.255.0",
    "no shutdown",
    "exit",
    "vlan 100",
    "name Automation_VLAN",
]

# Run the script
configure_devices(devices, commands)
```

Step 3: Test the Script

1. Run the script:

   bash

   python configure_devices.py

2. Verify the configuration:

   ○ Log into the devices manually or automate verification using Python:

   python

   connection.send_command("show running-config")

Output Example

Script Output:

plaintext

Connecting to 192.168.1.1...
Configuration pushed to 192.168.1.1:
interface GigabitEthernet0/1
 description Configured by Python Script
 ip address 192.168.100.1 255.255.255.0
 no shutdown
exit
vlan 100
 name Automation_VLAN
Configuration saved on 192.168.1.1.
Connecting to 192.168.1.2...
Configuration pushed to 192.168.1.2:
interface GigabitEthernet0/1
 description Configured by Python Script
 ip address 192.168.100.1 255.255.255.0

no shutdown

exit

vlan 100

name Automation_VLAN

Configuration saved on 192.168.1.2.

Device Configuration:

plaintext

interface GigabitEthernet0/1

description Configured by Python Script

ip address 192.168.100.1 255.255.255.0

no shutdown

!

vlan 100

name Automation_VLAN

4. Best Practices for Automating Device Configuration

1. **Test in a Controlled Environment**:
   - Use network simulators like GNS3 or Cisco VIRL for initial testing.
2. **Validate Device Reachability**:
   - Ensure devices are reachable before attempting configuration.

Example:

python

```
import os
response = os.system("ping -c 1 192.168.1.1")
if response == 0:
    print("Device is reachable")
```

3. **Use Logging**:

   o Log all script actions for troubleshooting and audit purposes.

   Example:

   python

```
import logging
logging.basicConfig(filename="automation.log", level=logging.INFO)
logging.info("Script started.")
```

4. **Implement Error Handling**:

   o Handle exceptions gracefully to avoid script crashes.

5. **Backup Configurations**:

   o Always back up the current configuration before applying changes.

Automating device configuration with Python and libraries like Paramiko and Netmiko can save significant time and effort while ensuring consistency and reducing human error. In this chapter, you learned how to automate login, execute commands, and push configuration changes across multiple devices.

In the next chapter, we'll explore **SNMP and Python**, focusing on how to query and monitor network devices programmatically. Let's continue automating and optimizing the network!

Chapter 9: SNMP and Python

SNMP (Simple Network Management Protocol) is a widely used protocol for network monitoring and management. It enables administrators to query devices for critical metrics, including bandwidth utilization, uptime, and performance data. In this chapter, we'll explore SNMP's fundamentals, use Python to query network devices, and provide a real-world example of monitoring bandwidth utilization.

1. Overview of SNMP for Network Monitoring

What Is SNMP?

SNMP is a protocol that facilitates communication between a **manager** (monitoring system) and **agents** (network devices).

- **Manager**: The monitoring system that queries or receives data from devices.
- **Agent**: The SNMP service running on network devices, which provides data to the manager.
- **MIB (Management Information Base)**: A hierarchical database of information available via SNMP.

- **OID (Object Identifier)**: A unique identifier for a piece of information in the MIB.

SNMP Operations

- **GET**: Retrieve data from a device.
- **SET**: Modify device settings (e.g., change thresholds).
- **TRAP**: Notify the manager of an event (e.g., device failure).
- **GETNEXT**: Retrieve the next item in the MIB tree.

SNMP Versions

- **v1**: Basic functionality, no encryption.
- **v2c**: Improved performance, still lacks encryption.
- **v3**: Adds authentication and encryption for security.

---

2. Using Python to Query Network Devices via SNMP

Python's pysnmp library provides a robust interface for working with SNMP.

Installing pysnmp
Install the library using pip:

bash

```
pip install pysnmp
```

Basic SNMP Query

The `getCmd` function in `pysnmp` is used for retrieving data from devices.

Example: Querying System Uptime:

python

```
from pysnmp.hlapi import *

# Define the SNMP target
target = "192.168.1.1"
community = "public"
oid = "1.3.6.1.2.1.1.3.0"  # sysUpTime

# Perform the SNMP GET operation
iterator = getCmd(
    SnmpEngine(),
    CommunityData(community, mpModel=0),  # SNMPv1
    UdpTransportTarget((target, 161)),
    ContextData(),
    ObjectType(ObjectIdentity(oid))
)

for errorIndication, errorStatus, errorIndex, varBinds in iterator:
    if errorIndication:
        print(f"Error: {errorIndication}")
    elif errorStatus:
        print(f"Error: {errorStatus.prettyPrint()}")
    else:
```

```
for varBind in varBinds:
    print(f"OID: {varBind[0]}, Value: {varBind[1]}")
```

Output:

plaintext

OID: 1.3.6.1.2.1.1.3.0, Value: 12345678

Retrieving Multiple SNMP Values

Use the nextCmd function to iterate through MIB objects.

Example: Querying Interface Descriptions:

python

```
from pysnmp.hlapi import *

target = "192.168.1.1"
community = "public"
oid = "1.3.6.1.2.1.2.2.1.2"  # ifDescr

iterator = nextCmd(
    SnmpEngine(),
    CommunityData(community, mpModel=0),  # SNMPv1
    UdpTransportTarget((target, 161)),
    ContextData(),
    ObjectType(ObjectIdentity(oid)),
    lexicographicMode=False
)
```

```
for errorIndication, errorStatus, errorIndex, varBinds in iterator:
    if errorIndication:
        print(f"Error: {errorIndication}")
    elif errorStatus:
        print(f"Error: {errorStatus.prettyPrint()}")
    else:
        for varBind in varBinds:
            print(f"OID: {varBind[0]}, Value: {varBind[1]}")
```

Output:

plaintext

OID: 1.3.6.1.2.1.2.2.1.2.1, Value: GigabitEthernet0/1
OID: 1.3.6.1.2.1.2.2.1.2.2, Value: GigabitEthernet0/2

3.   Real-World   Example: Monitoring   Bandwidth Utilization

Scenario

You want to monitor the bandwidth utilization on a router interface. The SNMP OIDs for incoming and outgoing traffic are:

- **InOctets**: 1.3.6.1.2.1.2.2.1.10.X (where X is the interface index).
- **OutOctets**: 1.3.6.1.2.1.2.2.1.16.X.

Python Script
Script: Bandwidth Monitoring

python

```python
import time
from pysnmp.hlapi import *

def get_snmp_value(target, community, oid):
    iterator = getCmd(
        SnmpEngine(),
        CommunityData(community, mpModel=0),  # SNMPv1
        UdpTransportTarget((target, 161)),
        ContextData(),
        ObjectType(ObjectIdentity(oid))
    )
    for errorIndication, errorStatus, errorIndex, varBinds in iterator:
        if errorIndication:
            print(f"Error: {errorIndication}")
            return None
        elif errorStatus:
            print(f"Error: {errorStatus.prettyPrint()}")
            return None
        else:
            for varBind in varBinds:
                return int(varBind[1])  # Return the value

def monitor_bandwidth(target, community, interface_index, interval=5):
    in_oid = f"1.3.6.1.2.1.2.2.1.10.{interface_index}"  # InOctets
    out_oid = f"1.3.6.1.2.1.2.2.1.16.{interface_index}"  # OutOctets

    print(f"Monitoring bandwidth on {target} (Interface {interface_index})")
    print("Press Ctrl+C to stop.\n")
    print("Time\t\tIncoming (bps)\tOutgoing (bps)")
```

```
try:
    while True:
        in1 = get_snmp_value(target, community, in_oid)
        out1 = get_snmp_value(target, community, out_oid)
        time.sleep(interval)
        in2 = get_snmp_value(target, community, in_oid)
        out2 = get_snmp_value(target, community, out_oid)

        # Calculate bandwidth in bits per second
        in_bps = ((in2 - in1) * 8) / interval
        out_bps = ((out2 - out1) * 8) / interval

        # Print results
        print(f"{time.strftime('%H:%M:%S')}\t{in_bps:.2f}\t\t{out_bps:.2f}")
    except KeyboardInterrupt:
        print("\nMonitoring stopped.")

# Example usage
monitor_bandwidth("192.168.1.1", "public", 1, interval=5)
```

How It Works

1. **SNMP Queries**:

   o The script queries InOctets and OutOctets twice, separated by a configurable interval.

2. **Calculate Bandwidth**:

o Bandwidth in bits per second is calculated using the formula:

plaintext

(CurrentOctets - PreviousOctets) * 8 / Interval

3. **Real-Time Monitoring**:
    o The script runs continuously, displaying live bandwidth statistics.

Output

plaintext

Monitoring bandwidth on 192.168.1.1 (Interface 1)
Press Ctrl+C to stop.

Time	Incoming (bps)	Outgoing (bps)
15:00:05	15000.00	8000.00
15:00:10	14000.00	9000.00
15:00:15	16000.00	7500.00

---

4. Best Practices for SNMP with Python

1. **Use SNMPv3 for Security**:

- o SNMPv1 and SNMPv2c lack encryption and are vulnerable to eavesdropping.
- o Use SNMPv3 for secure communication.

2. **Cache OIDs**:
   - o Avoid repeatedly fetching the same OID from devices to reduce network load.

3. **Handle Exceptions Gracefully**:
   - o Implement robust error handling for network timeouts or device unavailability.

4. **Limit Polling Frequency**:
   - o Polling too frequently can overwhelm the network or device CPU.

5. **Log Monitoring Data**:
   - o Store metrics in a database or file for long-term analysis.

This chapter introduced SNMP and its importance in network monitoring. You learned how to use Python's pysnmp library to query devices and monitor bandwidth utilization in real time. SNMP automation is a powerful tool for ensuring network performance and reliability.

In the next chapter, we'll explore **managing network inventory with Python**, focusing on how to build and maintain an automated inventory system for your network infrastructure. Let's continue enhancing your Python network automation skills!

Chapter 10: Managing Network Inventory with Python

Network inventory management is essential for maintaining a clear and accurate picture of the devices in your network. Python simplifies inventory management by enabling automation for device discovery, data storage, and real-time status checks. In this chapter, you'll learn how to store and retrieve device inventories using CSV and JSON, automate device discovery, and create a dynamic inventory system.

1. Storing and Retrieving Device Inventory

Using CSV for Inventory
CSV (Comma-Separated Values) is a simple and widely supported format for storing tabular data.

Example: Writing Inventory Data to a CSV File

python

import csv

Example inventory data

```
inventory = [
    {"hostname": "Router1", "ip": "192.168.1.1", "status": "active"},
    {"hostname": "Switch1", "ip": "192.168.1.2", "status": "inactive"},
]

# Write to CSV
with open("inventory.csv", "w", newline="") as csvfile:
    fieldnames = ["hostname", "ip", "status"]
    writer = csv.DictWriter(csvfile, fieldnames=fieldnames)

    writer.writeheader()
    writer.writerows(inventory)
```

Example: Reading Inventory Data from a CSV File

python

```
# Read from CSV
with open("inventory.csv", "r") as csvfile:
    reader = csv.DictReader(csvfile)
    for row in reader:
        print(row)
```

Using JSON for Inventory

JSON is ideal for structured data and supports hierarchical relationships.

Example: Writing Inventory Data to a JSON File

python

```
import json

# Example inventory data
inventory = [
    {"hostname": "Router1", "ip": "192.168.1.1", "status": "active"},
    {"hostname": "Switch1", "ip": "192.168.1.2", "status": "inactive"},
]

# Write to JSON
with open("inventory.json", "w") as jsonfile:
    json.dump(inventory, jsonfile, indent=4)
```

Example: Reading Inventory Data from a JSON File

python

```
# Read from JSON
with open("inventory.json", "r") as jsonfile:
    inventory = json.load(jsonfile)
    for device in inventory:
        print(device)
```

2. Automating Device Discovery and Status Checks

Device Discovery

You can automate device discovery using ping sweeps or SNMP.

Example: Discovering Devices in a Subnet

python

```python
import os

def discover_devices(subnet):
    active_devices = []
    for i in range(1, 255):  # Scan IP range 1-254
        ip = f"{subnet}.{i}"
        response = os.system(f"ping -c 1 {ip} > /dev/null 2>&1")
        if response == 0:
            active_devices.append(ip)
    return active_devices

# Example usage
subnet = "192.168.1"
devices = discover_devices(subnet)
print("Active devices:", devices)
```

Status Checks

You can use Python to query devices and check their operational status.

Example: Checking Device Reachability

python

```python
import socket

def check_device_status(ip, port=22):
    try:
        with socket.create_connection((ip, port), timeout=5):
            return True
```

```
except Exception:
    return False
```

```
# Example usage
devices = ["192.168.1.1", "192.168.1.2", "192.168.1.3"]
for device in devices:
    status = "reachable" if check_device_status(device) else "unreachable"
    print(f"{device} is {status}")
```

3. Creating a Dynamic Inventory for Network Devices

Scenario

You want to create a Python script that:

1. Discovers devices in a subnet.
2. Checks their reachability.
3. Stores the inventory in a JSON file.

Step 1: Device Discovery Use the discover_devices function from the previous section to scan a subnet.

Step 2: Status Checks Use the check_device_status function to verify device reachability.

Step 3: Store Inventory Write the discovered devices and their statuses to a JSON file.

Dynamic Inventory Script

python

```python
import os
import socket
import json

def discover_devices(subnet):
    active_devices = []
    for i in range(1, 255):  # Scan IP range 1-254
        ip = f"{subnet}.{i}"
        response = os.system(f"ping -c 1 {ip} > /dev/null 2>&1")
        if response == 0:
            active_devices.append(ip)
    return active_devices

def check_device_status(ip, port=22):
    try:
        with socket.create_connection((ip, port), timeout=5):
            return "reachable"
    except Exception:
        return "unreachable"

def create_inventory(subnet, output_file):
    devices = discover_devices(subnet)
    inventory = []
    for device in devices:
        status = check_device_status(device)
```

```python
        inventory.append({"ip": device, "status": status})

    # Save inventory to JSON
    with open(output_file, "w") as jsonfile:
        json.dump(inventory, jsonfile, indent=4)

    print(f"Inventory saved to {output_file}")

# Example usage
subnet = "192.168.1"
output_file = "dynamic_inventory.json"
create_inventory(subnet, output_file)
```

Output

dynamic_inventory.json:

json

```json
[
    {"ip": "192.168.1.1", "status": "reachable"},
    {"ip": "192.168.1.2", "status": "unreachable"},
    {"ip": "192.168.1.3", "status": "reachable"}
]
```

Console Output:

plaintext

```
Inventory saved to dynamic_inventory.json
```

4. Enhancing the Inventory System

Add Device Metadata

Include additional details like hostname and device type using SNMP or manual configuration.

Integrate with Network Monitoring Tools

Use APIs to fetch detailed data from monitoring tools like SolarWinds or Nagios.

Periodic Updates

Schedule the inventory script to run at regular intervals using a task scheduler (e.g., cron jobs or Windows Task Scheduler).

Web Interface

Build a web-based dashboard using Flask or Django to display the inventory dynamically.

This chapter demonstrated how to manage network inventories using Python. You learned to store and retrieve inventory data in CSV/JSON, automate device discovery and status checks, and create a dynamic inventory system. With these skills, you can streamline network management and maintain an accurate picture of your infrastructure.

In the next chapter, we'll explore **NAPALM for multi-vendor automation**, focusing on simplifying network tasks across diverse environments. Let's continue building efficient network automation solutions!

Chapter 11: Using NAPALM for Multi-Vendor Automation

Managing a network with devices from multiple vendors can be challenging due to variations in configuration interfaces and commands. **NAPALM (Network Automation and Programmability Abstraction Layer with Multivendor support)** simplifies this complexity by providing a unified API to interact with various network devices. In this chapter, you'll learn about NAPALM, explore examples of retrieving and configuring device data, and implement a real-world use case for standardizing configurations across vendors.

1. Introduction to NAPALM

What is NAPALM?

NAPALM is a Python library designed to abstract the complexities of interacting with network devices. It supports various vendors, including Cisco, Juniper, Arista, and more.

Why Use NAPALM?

1. **Unified Interface**:

o A single API for interacting with devices from different vendors.

2. **Ease of Use**:
   o Simplifies common tasks like retrieving configuration, managing interfaces, and pushing configurations.

3. **Extensive Support**:
   o Supports major vendors like Cisco, Juniper, Arista, and Huawei.

4. **Community-Driven**:
   o Open-source with active contributions and support.

Supported Functions

- **Getters**: Retrieve information like interfaces, routing tables, and ARP tables.
- **Configuration Management**: Push and validate configurations.
- **Operational Tasks**: Manage interfaces, check device health, and more.

Installing NAPALM

Install NAPALM using pip:

bash

```
pip install napalm
```

2. Examples of Retrieving and Configuring Device Data

Connecting to a Device

To connect to a device, you need the following:

- **Driver**: Specific to the device vendor (e.g., ios, junos).
- **Connection Details**: IP address, username, and password.

Example: Connecting to a Cisco Device

python

```python
from napalm import get_network_driver

# Define device credentials
device_details = {
    "hostname": "192.168.1.1",
    "username": "admin",
    "password": "password",
}

# Load the driver for Cisco IOS
driver = get_network_driver("ios")

# Establish a connection
device = driver(**device_details)
device.open()
```

```python
print(f"Connected to {device_details['hostname']}")
device.close()
```

Retrieving Device Data

NAPALM provides a set of **getters** to retrieve various device details.

Example: Getting Device Facts

python

```python
device.open()
facts = device.get_facts()
device.close()

print("Device Facts:")
print(f"Hostname: {facts['hostname']}")
print(f"Model: {facts['model']}")
print(f"Uptime: {facts['uptime']} seconds")
```

Output:

plaintext

```
Device Facts:
Hostname: Router1
Model: ISR4451
Uptime: 1023400 seconds
```

Example: Retrieving Interfaces

python

```
device.open()
interfaces = device.get_interfaces()
device.close()

print("Interfaces:")
for interface, details in interfaces.items():
    print(f"{interface}: {details}")
```

Output:

plaintext

```
Interfaces:
GigabitEthernet0/1: {'is_up': True, 'is_enabled': True, 'description': '', ...}
GigabitEthernet0/2: {'is_up': False, 'is_enabled': True, 'description': '', ...}
```

Pushing Configuration

You can push configurations to devices using NAPALM's load_merge_candidate() method.

Example: Adding an Interface Description

python

```
config = """
interface GigabitEthernet0/1
 description Configured by NAPALM
"""

device.open()
device.load_merge_candidate(config=config)
```

```python
# Commit the configuration
device.commit_config()
device.close()

print("Configuration pushed successfully!")
```

Validating Configuration

NAPALM allows you to validate configurations before committing them.

Example: Testing a Configuration

```python
python

device.open()
device.load_merge_candidate(config="interface    Loopback0\n    ip    address
192.168.1.1 255.255.255.0")

# Compare the candidate configuration with the running configuration
diff = device.compare_config()
if diff:
    print("Changes to be applied:")
    print(diff)
    device.commit_config()
else:
    print("No changes needed.")
device.close()
```

---

3. Real-World Use Case: Standardizing Configurations Across Vendors

Scenario

You need to standardize VLAN configurations across devices from multiple vendors, ensuring consistency in naming and assignments.

Script: Standardizing VLANs

Step 1: Define Device Inventory Create a list of devices with their connection details and drivers.

python

```
devices = [
    {"driver": "ios", "hostname": "192.168.1.1", "username": "admin",
"password": "password"},
    {"driver": "junos", "hostname": "192.168.1.2", "username": "admin",
"password": "password"},
]
```

Step 2: Define VLAN Configuration Specify the VLAN configuration to be applied.

python

```
vlan_config = """
vlan 100
```

```
 name Standard_VLAN
"""
```

Step 3: Create the Automation Script The script connects to each device, applies the VLAN configuration, and validates the changes.

python

```python
from napalm import get_network_driver

def standardize_vlans(devices, vlan_config):
    for device_info in devices:
        try:
            print(f"Connecting to {device_info['hostname']}...")

            # Load the driver and connect to the device
            driver = get_network_driver(device_info["driver"])
            device = driver(
                hostname=device_info["hostname"],
                username=device_info["username"],
                password=device_info["password"],
            )
            device.open()

            # Push the VLAN configuration
            print(f"Applying configuration to {device_info['hostname']}...")
            device.load_merge_candidate(config=vlan_config)

            # Compare and commit changes
            diff = device.compare_config()
```

```
        if diff:
            print(f"Changes for {device_info['hostname']}:\n{diff}")
            device.commit_config()
            print(f"Configuration applied to {device_info['hostname']}.")
        else:
            print(f"No changes needed for {device_info['hostname']}.")

        device.close()
    except Exception as e:
        print(f"Error configuring {device_info['hostname']}: {e}")

# Run the script
standardize_vlans(devices, vlan_config)
```

Output

plaintext

```
Connecting to 192.168.1.1...
Applying configuration to 192.168.1.1...
Changes for 192.168.1.1:
vlan 100
 name Standard_VLAN
Configuration applied to 192.168.1.1.
Connecting to 192.168.1.2...
Applying configuration to 192.168.1.2...
Changes for 192.168.1.2:
set vlans 100 description Standard_VLAN
Configuration applied to 192.168.1.2.
```

4. Best Practices for Using NAPALM

1. **Test in a Lab Environment**:
   - Validate scripts in a controlled lab before deploying to production.

2. **Backup Configurations**:
   - Use NAPALM's get_config() to back up running configurations.

   Example:

   python

   ```python
   config = device.get_config()["running"]
   with open("backup_config.txt", "w") as file:
       file.write(config)
   ```

3. **Use Version Control**:
   - Track configuration changes using version control tools like Git.

4. **Implement Logging**:
   - Log actions and results for troubleshooting and audits.

   Example:

   python

   ```python
   import logging
   ```

logging.basicConfig(filename="automation.log", level=logging.INFO)

5. **Monitor Device Compatibility**:

   o Ensure all devices are supported by NAPALM's drivers.

NAPALM is a powerful tool for simplifying multi-vendor network automation. It provides a consistent API for interacting with diverse devices, enabling efficient configuration management and monitoring. In this chapter, you learned how to retrieve and configure device data using NAPALM, culminating in a practical example of standardizing VLAN configurations across vendors.

In the next chapter, we'll explore **Python and Network Security**, focusing on automating security tasks like managing ACLs and detecting vulnerabilities. Let's continue advancing your network automation skills!

Chapter 12: Python and Network Security

Network security is critical in today's interconnected world. With Python, network engineers can automate tedious security tasks, detect vulnerabilities, and implement safeguards to protect network infrastructure. This chapter explores how to use Python to automate security-related tasks such as updating passwords, managing ACLs, and deploying firewall rules. You'll also learn to identify and mitigate vulnerabilities programmatically.

---

1. Automating Security Tasks

Updating Device Passwords
Automating password updates ensures consistency and reduces the risk of weak or outdated credentials.

Example: Updating Device Passwords with Netmiko

python

```
from netmiko import ConnectHandler

def update_passwords(devices, new_password):
```

```python
for device in devices:
    try:
        print(f"Connecting to {device['host']}...")
        connection = ConnectHandler(**device)

        # Update password command
        commands = [
            f"username {device['username']} secret {new_password}",
            "write memory"
        ]
        connection.send_config_set(commands)
        print(f"Password updated for {device['host']}")
        connection.disconnect()
    except Exception as e:
        print(f"Error updating password for {device['host']}: {e}")


# Example usage
devices = [
    {"device_type": "cisco_ios", "host": "192.168.1.1", "username": "admin",
"password": "old_password"},
    {"device_type": "cisco_ios", "host": "192.168.1.2", "username": "admin",
"password": "old_password"},
]
update_passwords(devices, "new_secure_password")
```

Managing ACLs

Access Control Lists (ACLs) are essential for filtering traffic and securing the network. Automating ACL management can help ensure that the rules are consistent across devices.

Example: Automating ACL Updates

python

```python
def update_acl(device, acl_commands):
    try:
        connection = ConnectHandler(**device)
        print(f"Updating ACL on {device['host']}...")
        connection.send_config_set(acl_commands)
        connection.send_command("write memory")
        print(f"ACL updated on {device['host']}.")
        connection.disconnect()
    except Exception as e:
        print(f"Error updating ACL on {device['host']}: {e}")


# Example usage
device = {"device_type": "cisco_ios", "host": "192.168.1.1", "username": "admin", "password": "password"}
acl_commands = [
    "ip access-list extended ACL_SECURE",
    "permit tcp any any eq 80",
    "permit tcp any any eq 443",
    "deny ip any any log"
]
update_acl(device, acl_commands)
```

2. Using Python to Detect and Mitigate Vulnerabilities

Detecting Vulnerabilities

Python can be used to scan devices for known vulnerabilities or weak configurations.

Example: Checking for Weak Passwords

python

```
import paramiko

def check_weak_password(host, username, weak_passwords):
    for password in weak_passwords:
        try:
            ssh = paramiko.SSHClient()
            ssh.set_missing_host_key_policy(paramiko.AutoAddPolicy())
            ssh.connect(hostname=host, username=username, password=password,
timeout=5)
            print(f"Weak password found for {host}: {password}")
            ssh.close()
            return
        except:
            continue
    print(f"No weak passwords found for {host}")

# Example usage
weak_passwords = ["1234", "password", "admin", "cisco"]
check_weak_password("192.168.1.1", "admin", weak_passwords)
```

Mitigating Vulnerabilities

Once vulnerabilities are detected, Python scripts can automatically apply fixes.

Example: Disabling Unused Interfaces

python

```python
def disable_unused_interfaces(device, interfaces):
    try:
        connection = ConnectHandler(**device)
        for interface in interfaces:
            commands = [f"interface {interface}", "shutdown"]
            connection.send_config_set(commands)
        connection.send_command("write memory")
        print(f"Unused interfaces disabled on {device['host']}")
        connection.disconnect()
    except Exception as e:
        print(f"Error disabling interfaces on {device['host']}: {e}")

# Example usage
device = {"device_type": "cisco_ios", "host": "192.168.1.1", "username": "admin", "password": "password"}
unused_interfaces = ["GigabitEthernet0/2", "GigabitEthernet0/3"]
disable_unused_interfaces(device, unused_interfaces)
```

3. Real-World Example: Automating Firewall Rules Deployment

Scenario

You need to deploy a set of firewall rules across multiple devices to block unauthorized access to critical servers.

Step 1: Define the Firewall Rules

python

```python
firewall_rules = [
    "ip access-list extended BLOCK_CRITICAL",
    "deny ip any host 10.0.0.10 log",
    "deny ip any host 10.0.0.11 log",
    "permit ip any any",
]
```

Step 2: Define the Deployment Script

python

```python
from netmiko import ConnectHandler

def deploy_firewall_rules(devices, rules):
    for device in devices:
        try:
            print(f"Deploying firewall rules to {device['host']}...")
            connection = ConnectHandler(**device)
            connection.send_config_set(rules)
            connection.send_command("write memory")
            print(f"Firewall rules deployed to {device['host']}")
```

```
        connection.disconnect()
    except Exception as e:
        print(f"Error deploying firewall rules to {device['host']}: {e}")


# Example usage
devices = [
    {"device_type": "cisco_ios", "host": "192.168.1.1", "username": "admin",
"password": "password"},
    {"device_type": "cisco_ios", "host": "192.168.1.2", "username": "admin",
"password": "password"},
]
deploy_firewall_rules(devices, firewall_rules)
```

Step 3: Run the Script Execute the script to deploy the rules across the devices:

bash

```
python deploy_firewall_rules.py
```

Output:

plaintext

```
Deploying firewall rules to 192.168.1.1...
Firewall rules deployed to 192.168.1.1
Deploying firewall rules to 192.168.1.2...
Firewall rules deployed to 192.168.1.2
```

4. Best Practices for Python and Network Security

1. **Use Secure Protocols**:

   o Use SSH for secure communication and SNMPv3 for monitoring.

2. **Backup Configurations**:

   o Always back up configurations before making changes.

3. **Test in a Lab Environment**:

   o Validate scripts in a simulated environment before applying them in production.

4. **Log Actions**:

   o Maintain logs for all automated actions for audit and troubleshooting purposes.

Example:

python

```
import logging
logging.basicConfig(filename="security_automation.log",
level=logging.INFO)
logging.info("Firewall rules deployed.")
```

5. **Implement Role-Based Access Control (RBAC)**:

   o Limit access to scripts and devices based on user roles.

Python is a powerful tool for automating network security tasks, reducing the likelihood of human error, and improving response times to vulnerabilities. In this chapter, you learned how to automate password updates, manage ACLs, detect vulnerabilities, and deploy firewall rules programmatically.

In the next chapter, we'll explore **Configuring VLANs and Subnets with Python**, focusing on automating network segmentation tasks to enhance performance and security. Let's continue streamlining network operations!

Chapter 13: Configuring VLANs and Subnets with Python

Network segmentation through VLANs (Virtual Local Area Networks) and subnetting is a cornerstone of efficient and secure network design. Automating these tasks with Python ensures consistency and reduces configuration time, especially in large-scale networks. In this chapter, you'll learn how to automate VLAN and subnet assignments using Python, with a practical example of deploying VLAN configurations across multiple switches.

---

1. Automating VLAN and Subnet Assignments

What Are VLANs and Subnets?

- **VLANs**:
    - Logical segmentation of networks at Layer 2.
    - Devices in the same VLAN can communicate as if they were on the same physical network.
    - Example: VLAN 10 for employees, VLAN 20 for guests.
- **Subnets**:
    - Logical division of networks at Layer 3.

- o Each subnet is associated with a unique range of IP addresses.
- o Example: 192.168.10.0/24 for VLAN 10, 192.168.20.0/24 for VLAN 20.

Why Automate VLAN and Subnet Assignments?

- **Consistency**:
  - o Ensures VLAN IDs and subnet assignments are consistent across all switches and routers.
- **Scalability**:
  - o Handles configurations for multiple devices efficiently.
- **Error Reduction**:
  - o Minimizes human error in repetitive tasks.

2. Using Python to Configure VLANs

Automating VLAN Creation

The example below demonstrates how to use Netmiko to automate VLAN configuration on a Cisco switch.

Example: Create VLANs

python

```python
from netmiko import ConnectHandler

def create_vlans(device, vlan_config):
    try:
        print(f"Connecting to {device['host']}...")
        connection = ConnectHandler(**device)
        connection.send_config_set(vlan_config)
        connection.send_command("write memory")
        print(f"VLANs configured on {device['host']}")
        connection.disconnect()
    except Exception as e:
        print(f"Error configuring VLANs on {device['host']}: {e}")

# Example usage
device = {"device_type": "cisco_ios", "host": "192.168.1.1", "username":
"admin", "password": "password"}
vlan_config = [
    "vlan 10",
    "name Employees",
    "vlan 20",
    "name Guests"
]
create_vlans(device, vlan_config)
```

Output:

plaintext

Connecting to 192.168.1.1...

VLANs configured on 192.168.1.1

Assigning VLANs to Interfaces

You can automate assigning VLANs to specific switch interfaces.

Example: Assign VLAN to Interfaces

python

```python
def assign_vlan_to_interface(device, interface, vlan_id):
    try:
        print(f"Assigning VLAN {vlan_id} to {interface} on {device['host']}...")
        connection = ConnectHandler(**device)
        commands = [
            f"interface {interface}",
            f"switchport mode access",
            f"switchport access vlan {vlan_id}"
        ]
        connection.send_config_set(commands)
        connection.send_command("write memory")
        print(f"VLAN {vlan_id} assigned to {interface} on {device['host']}")
        connection.disconnect()
    except Exception as e:
        print(f"Error assigning VLAN to interface on {device['host']}: {e}")

# Example usage
assign_vlan_to_interface(device, "GigabitEthernet0/1", 10)
```

Output:

plaintext

```
Assigning VLAN 10 to GigabitEthernet0/1 on 192.168.1.1...
VLAN 10 assigned to GigabitEthernet0/1 on 192.168.1.1
```

3. Automating Subnet Assignments

Defining Subnet Ranges

Each VLAN is assigned a corresponding subnet. Automating this ensures correct IP address assignments.

Example: Define Subnet Ranges

python

```
vlans = [
    {"vlan_id": 10, "name": "Employees", "subnet": "192.168.10.0/24"},
    {"vlan_id": 20, "name": "Guests", "subnet": "192.168.20.0/24"}
]

for vlan in vlans:
    print(f"VLAN {vlan['vlan_id']} ({vlan['name']}) is assigned to subnet {vlan['subnet']}")
```

Output:

plaintext

```
VLAN 10 (Employees) is assigned to subnet 192.168.10.0/24
VLAN 20 (Guests) is assigned to subnet 192.168.20.0/24
```

Configuring Subnet on a Router

Use Python to configure the VLAN interface with the appropriate subnet.

Example: Configure VLAN Subnet on Router

python

```python
def configure_vlan_subnet(device, vlan_id, subnet, mask):
    try:
        print(f"Configuring VLAN {vlan_id} with subnet {subnet} on {device['host']}...")
        connection = ConnectHandler(**device)
        commands = [
            f"interface vlan {vlan_id}",
            f"ip address {subnet} {mask}",
            "no shutdown"
        ]
        connection.send_config_set(commands)
        connection.send_command("write memory")
        print(f"VLAN {vlan_id} subnet configured on {device['host']}")
        connection.disconnect()
    except Exception as e:
        print(f"Error configuring VLAN subnet on {device['host']}: {e}")

# Example usage
configure_vlan_subnet(device, 10, "192.168.10.1", "255.255.255.0")
```

Output:

plaintext

Configuring VLAN 10 with subnet 192.168.10.0 on 192.168.1.1...
VLAN 10 subnet configured on 192.168.1.1

4. Example: Deploying VLAN Configurations Across Multiple Switches

Scenario

Deploy the following VLANs across multiple switches:

- VLAN 10: Employees (192.168.10.0/24)
- VLAN 20: Guests (192.168.20.0/24)

Script: Deploy VLAN Configurations

python

```
from netmiko import ConnectHandler

def deploy_vlans(devices, vlans):
    for device in devices:
        try:
            print(f"Connecting to {device['host']}...")
            connection = ConnectHandler(**device)

            for vlan in vlans:
                commands = [
                    f"vlan {vlan['vlan_id']}",
                    f"name {vlan['name']}",
                    f"interface vlan {vlan['vlan_id']}",
                    f"ip address {vlan['gateway']} {vlan['mask']}",
                    "no shutdown"
                ]
```

```
        connection.send_config_set(commands)

      connection.send_command("write memory")
      print(f"VLANs configured on {device['host']}")
      connection.disconnect()
    except Exception as e:
      print(f"Error configuring VLANs on {device['host']}: {e}")

# Define devices and VLANs
devices = [
    {"device_type": "cisco_ios", "host": "192.168.1.1", "username": "admin",
"password": "password"},
    {"device_type": "cisco_ios", "host": "192.168.1.2", "username": "admin",
"password": "password"}
]

vlans = [
    {"vlan_id": 10, "name": "Employees", "gateway": "192.168.10.1", "mask":
"255.255.255.0"},
    {"vlan_id": 20, "name": "Guests", "gateway": "192.168.20.1", "mask":
"255.255.255.0"}
]

# Deploy VLANs
deploy_vlans(devices, vlans)
```

Output

plaintext

Connecting to 192.168.1.1...

VLANs configured on 192.168.1.1

Connecting to 192.168.1.2...

VLANs configured on 192.168.1.2

5. Best Practices for VLAN and Subnet Automation

1. **Validate VLAN IDs and Subnets**:
   - Ensure VLAN IDs and subnets are unique across the network.

2. **Backup Configurations**:
   - Back up device configurations before deploying changes.

3. **Use Templates**:
   - Create reusable configuration templates for consistency.

4. **Test in a Lab Environment**:
   - Test scripts in a controlled environment before deploying to production.

5. **Log Changes**:
   - Maintain logs for audit and troubleshooting purposes.

Python simplifies the deployment and management of VLANs and subnets, ensuring consistency and efficiency across network devices. In this chapter, you learned to automate VLAN creation, assign subnets, and deploy configurations across multiple switches using Python. These skills are essential for scaling network operations and improving security.

In the next chapter, we'll explore **Python and Network Monitoring**, focusing on automating tasks like real-time performance monitoring and generating reports. Let's continue building robust network automation solutions!

Chapter 14: Python and Network Monitoring

Effective network monitoring is critical for maintaining optimal performance and ensuring minimal downtime. Python provides powerful tools for monitoring network health, generating performance reports, and automating alerts for performance issues. In this chapter, you'll learn to monitor key metrics like latency, bandwidth, and uptime, generate performance reports, and implement a real-world example of automating alerts for performance degradation.

1. Generating Network Performance Reports

Key Metrics for Network Performance

- **Latency**: The time it takes for data to travel between two points.
- **Bandwidth**: The amount of data transmitted over a network in a specific time frame.
- **Uptime**: The duration a device or network is operational.

Example: Generating a Performance Report

Script:

python

```python
import csv
import time
from datetime import datetime
import subprocess

# List of devices to monitor
devices = [
    {"hostname": "Router1", "ip": "192.168.1.1"},
    {"hostname": "Switch1", "ip": "192.168.1.2"}
]

# Function to check latency
def check_latency(ip):
    try:
        result = subprocess.run(["ping", "-c", "1", ip], stdout=subprocess.PIPE, text=True)
        output = result.stdout
        latency_line = [line for line in output.split("\n") if "time=" in line]
        if latency_line:
            latency = latency_line[0].split("time=")[-1].split(" ")[0]
            return float(latency)
        return None
    except Exception as e:
        print(f"Error checking latency for {ip}: {e}")
        return None

# Generate a performance report
```

```python
def generate_report(devices, output_file):
    with open(output_file, "w", newline="") as csvfile:
        fieldnames = ["Timestamp", "Hostname", "IP", "Latency (ms)"]
        writer = csv.DictWriter(csvfile, fieldnames=fieldnames)
        writer.writeheader()

        for device in devices:
            latency = check_latency(device["ip"])
            writer.writerow({
                "Timestamp": datetime.now().strftime("%Y-%m-%d %H:%M:%S"),
                "Hostname": device["hostname"],
                "IP": device["ip"],
                "Latency (ms)": latency if latency is not None else "N/A"
            })
    print(f"Report saved to {output_file}")

# Generate the report
generate_report(devices, "network_performance_report.csv")
```

Output (CSV File):

plaintext

```
Timestamp,Hostname,IP,Latency (ms)
2025-01-04 15:00:00,Router1,192.168.1.1,5.2
2025-01-04 15:00:00,Switch1,192.168.1.2,8.6
```

2. Monitoring Latency, Bandwidth, and Uptime

Monitoring Latency

Latency can be monitored using Python and the ping command, as shown above.

Monitoring Bandwidth

Bandwidth usage can be retrieved using SNMP.

Example: Monitoring Bandwidth Utilization

python

```
from pysnmp.hlapi import *

def get_bandwidth(ip, community, oid):
    iterator = getCmd(
        SnmpEngine(),
        CommunityData(community, mpModel=0),  # SNMPv1
        UdpTransportTarget((ip, 161)),
        ContextData(),
        ObjectType(ObjectIdentity(oid))
    )

    for errorIndication, errorStatus, errorIndex, varBinds in iterator:
        if errorIndication:
            print(f"Error: {errorIndication}")
            return None
        elif errorStatus:
            print(f"Error: {errorStatus.prettyPrint()}")
            return None
        else:
```

```
    for varBind in varBinds:
        return int(varBind[1])  # Return the value
```

```
# Example usage
in_octets_oid = "1.3.6.1.2.1.2.2.1.10.1"  # Replace with correct OID for InOctets
out_octets_oid  =  "1.3.6.1.2.1.2.2.1.16.1"   #  Replace  with  correct  OID  for
OutOctets
```

```
ip = "192.168.1.1"
community = "public"
```

```
in_bandwidth = get_bandwidth(ip, community, in_octets_oid)
out_bandwidth = get_bandwidth(ip, community, out_octets_oid)
print(f"In Bandwidth: {in_bandwidth} bytes, Out Bandwidth: {out_bandwidth}
bytes")
```

Monitoring Uptime

Uptime can be retrieved via SNMP or commands like show version
for Cisco devices.

Example: Checking Uptime via SNMP

python

```
uptime_oid = "1.3.6.1.2.1.1.3.0"  # sysUpTime OID
uptime = get_bandwidth(ip, community, uptime_oid)
print(f"Device Uptime: {uptime} ticks")
```

3. Real-World Example: Automating Alerts for Performance Degradation

Scenario

You need to monitor network devices for high latency and send email alerts when thresholds are exceeded.

Script: Automating Alerts
Step 1: Define Monitoring Function

python

```python
import smtplib
from email.mime.text import MIMEText

# Send an email alert
def send_alert(device, metric, value, threshold):
    sender = "alerts@example.com"
    recipient = "admin@example.com"
    subject = f"Performance Alert: {device['hostname']}"
    body = (
        f"Alert: {metric} for {device['hostname']} ({device['ip']}) has exceeded the
threshold.\n"
        f"Current Value: {value}\n"
        f"Threshold: {threshold}\n"
    )

    msg = MIMEText(body)
```

```python
msg["Subject"] = subject
msg["From"] = sender
msg["To"] = recipient

with smtplib.SMTP("smtp.example.com", 587) as server:
    server.starttls()
    server.login("alerts@example.com", "password")
    server.sendmail(sender, recipient, msg.as_string())
print(f"Alert sent for {device['hostname']}")
```

Step 2: Monitor Devices

python

```python
def monitor_devices(devices, latency_threshold):
    for device in devices:
        latency = check_latency(device["ip"])
        if latency and latency > latency_threshold:
            send_alert(device, "Latency", latency, latency_threshold)
        else:
            print(f"{device['hostname']} is performing normally.")
```

Step 3: Run the Monitoring Script

python

```python
devices = [
    {"hostname": "Router1", "ip": "192.168.1.1"},
    {"hostname": "Switch1", "ip": "192.168.1.2"}
]

latency_threshold = 100  # Milliseconds
monitor_devices(devices, latency_threshold)
```

Output

- **Console**:

plaintext

Router1 is performing normally.
Switch1 is performing normally.

- **Email Alert**:

plaintext

Subject: Performance Alert: Router1

Alert: Latency for Router1 (192.168.1.1) has exceeded the threshold.
Current Value: 120 ms
Threshold: 100 ms

4. Best Practices for Network Monitoring Automation

1. **Set Realistic Thresholds**:
   - Define thresholds for metrics like latency and bandwidth based on historical performance data.
2. **Log Monitoring Data**:

o Store performance data in logs or databases for long-term analysis.

3. **Secure Alerts**:

   o Use secure email protocols (e.g., SMTP with TLS) for sending alerts.

4. **Integrate with Monitoring Tools**:

   o Extend scripts to work with monitoring tools like Nagios, Zabbix, or SolarWinds.

5. **Test Alerts**:

   o Regularly test the alert system to ensure timely notifications.

Python is an excellent tool for automating network monitoring tasks. In this chapter, you learned to generate network performance reports, monitor latency, bandwidth, and uptime, and implement a real-world example of automated alerts for performance degradation. These skills are essential for maintaining network reliability and responding proactively to potential issues.

In the next chapter, we'll explore **Managing IP Address Allocations with Python**, focusing on automating IP management tasks and creating a simple IP address allocation tool. Let's continue enhancing your network automation expertise!

Chapter 15: Python for Device Backups and Restorations

Backing up network device configurations is a critical task for maintaining operational integrity and ensuring rapid disaster recovery. Python provides tools to automate backups, manage configuration files, and streamline the restoration process. In this chapter, you'll learn to automate device configuration backups, implement disaster recovery processes, and create a periodic automated backup system for network devices.

1. Automating Backup of Device Configurations

Why Automate Backups?

- **Consistency**: Ensures configurations are regularly backed up without manual intervention.
- **Time-Saving**: Reduces the time spent on repetitive tasks.
- **Rapid Recovery**: Speeds up restoration in case of a device failure.

Using Python to Retrieve Configurations

Libraries like **Netmiko** and **Paramiko** enable SSH-based automation for retrieving device configurations.

Example: Backing Up Configurations with Netmiko

python

```
from netmiko import ConnectHandler

def backup_device_config(device, backup_dir):
    try:
        print(f"Connecting to {device['host']}...")
        connection = ConnectHandler(**device)

        # Fetch the running configuration
        config = connection.send_command("show running-config")

        # Save the configuration to a file
        backup_file = f"{backup_dir}/{device['host']}_backup.txt"
        with open(backup_file, "w") as file:
            file.write(config)
        print(f"Backup saved for {device['host']} at {backup_file}")

        connection.disconnect()
    except Exception as e:
        print(f"Error backing up configuration for {device['host']}: {e}")

# Example usage
```

```
device = {"device_type": "cisco_ios", "host": "192.168.1.1", "username":
"admin", "password": "password"}
backup_device_config(device, "backups")
```

Output:

plaintext

Connecting to 192.168.1.1...
Backup saved for 192.168.1.1 at backups/192.168.1.1_backup.txt

---

2. Using Python for Disaster Recovery and Configuration Restoration

Restoring Configurations

Python scripts can restore configurations by pushing them to devices via SSH.

Example: Restoring a Configuration

python

```python
def restore_device_config(device, config_file):
    try:
        print(f"Restoring configuration on {device['host']}...")
        connection = ConnectHandler(**device)

        # Load configuration from the file
        with open(config_file, "r") as file:
            config_lines = file.readlines()
```

```
    # Push the configuration to the device
    connection.send_config_set(config_lines)
    connection.send_command("write memory")
    print(f"Configuration restored on {device['host']}")

    connection.disconnect()
  except Exception as e:
    print(f"Error restoring configuration for {device['host']}: {e}")

# Example usage
restore_device_config(device, "backups/192.168.1.1_backup.txt")
```

Output:

```plaintext
Restoring configuration on 192.168.1.1...
Configuration restored on 192.168.1.1
```

3. Example: Periodic Automated Backups for Network Devices

Scenario

You need to back up device configurations daily to ensure up-to-date configurations are available for disaster recovery.

Automated Backup Script

```python
python

import os
from datetime import datetime
from netmiko import ConnectHandler

def backup_device_configs(devices, backup_dir):
    # Ensure backup directory exists
    os.makedirs(backup_dir, exist_ok=True)

    for device in devices:
        try:
            print(f"Connecting to {device['host']}...")
            connection = ConnectHandler(**device)

            # Fetch the running configuration
            config = connection.send_command("show running-config")

            # Save the configuration with a timestamp
            timestamp = datetime.now().strftime("%Y%m%d_%H%M%S")
            backup_file = f"{backup_dir}/{device['host']}_backup_{timestamp}.txt"
            with open(backup_file, "w") as file:
                file.write(config)
            print(f"Backup saved for {device['host']} at {backup_file}")

            connection.disconnect()
        except Exception as e:
            print(f"Error backing up configuration for {device['host']}: {e}")

# Define devices and backup directory
```

```
devices = [
    {"device_type": "cisco_ios", "host": "192.168.1.1", "username": "admin",
"password": "password"},
    {"device_type": "cisco_ios", "host": "192.168.1.2", "username": "admin",
"password": "password"}
]
backup_dir = "daily_backups"

# Run the backup script
backup_device_configs(devices, backup_dir)
```

Scheduling the Backup

Use a task scheduler to run the script periodically:

- **Linux**: Schedule with cron.

    bash

    0 2 * * * python /path/to/backup_script.py

- **Windows**: Use Task Scheduler to run the script daily.

4. Best Practices for Device Backups and Restorations

1. **Secure Storage**:

> o Store backups in a secure, centralized location, such as a network-attached storage (NAS) or cloud storage.

2. **Encrypt Backups**:

> o Use encryption to protect sensitive configuration data.

Example:

bash

openssl aes-256-cbc -in backup.txt -out backup.txt.enc -k password

3. **Version Control**:

> o Keep multiple versions of backups for historical tracking and rollback purposes.

4. **Monitor Backup Status**:

> o Log backup results and implement alerts for failed backups.

Example:

python

```
import logging
logging.basicConfig(filename="backup.log", level=logging.INFO)
logging.info("Backup completed successfully.")
```

5. **Test Restorations**:

o Periodically test restoration processes to ensure backups are functional.

Automating device backups and restorations with Python is essential for ensuring network resilience and minimizing downtime during disasters. In this chapter, you learned how to automate configuration backups, implement restoration processes, and create a periodic backup system for multiple devices. These skills are vital for maintaining a secure and well-managed network.

In the next chapter, we'll explore **Python and Software-Defined Networking (SDN)**, focusing on automating and managing SDN-based architectures for enhanced scalability and flexibility. Let's continue enhancing your network automation capabilities!

Chapter 16: Automating Software Upgrades

Keeping network devices up to date with the latest firmware is crucial for security, stability, and performance. Automating firmware upgrades with Python reduces manual effort, minimizes downtime, and ensures consistency across devices. This chapter explores how to use Python to manage firmware upgrades and provides a real-world example of rolling out updates across a network.

1. Using Python to Manage Firmware Upgrades

Why Automate Firmware Upgrades?

1. **Efficiency**: Upgrading devices in bulk saves time.
2. **Consistency**: Ensures all devices are updated to the same firmware version.
3. **Error Reduction**: Reduces the risk of human error during upgrades.
4. **Security**: Ensures vulnerabilities are patched in a timely manner.

Key Steps in Firmware Upgrades

1. **Backup Configurations**:
   - Always back up device configurations before starting the upgrade.
2. **Upload Firmware**:
   - Transfer the firmware image to the device.
3. **Apply the Upgrade**:
   - Install the firmware and reboot the device.
4. **Verify the Upgrade**:
   - Check the device version to confirm the upgrade.

2. Automating Firmware Upload and Upgrade

Uploading Firmware Using Python
Python libraries like **Netmiko** and **Paramiko** enable automated file transfers and remote execution of upgrade commands.

Example: Uploading Firmware with Netmiko

python

```
from netmiko import ConnectHandler
from netmiko import file_transfer
```

```python
def upload_firmware(device, source_file, dest_file):
    try:
        print(f"Connecting to {device['host']}...")
        connection = ConnectHandler(**device)

        # Transfer the firmware file
        transfer_result = file_transfer(
            connection,
            source_file=source_file,
            dest_file=dest_file,
            file_system="flash:",
            overwrite_file=True
        )

        if transfer_result["file_transferred"]:
            print(f"Firmware uploaded to {device['host']} successfully.")
        else:
            print(f"Firmware upload failed on {device['host']}.")

        connection.disconnect()
    except Exception as e:
        print(f"Error uploading firmware to {device['host']}: {e}")

# Example usage
device = {
    "device_type": "cisco_ios",
    "host": "192.168.1.1",
    "username": "admin",
    "password": "password"
}
```

upload_firmware(device, "ios_image.bin", "ios_image.bin")

Applying the Upgrade

Once the firmware is uploaded, you can automate the upgrade and reboot process.

Example: Applying the Upgrade

python

```python
def apply_firmware_upgrade(device, firmware_file):
    try:
        print(f"Upgrading firmware on {device['host']}...")
        connection = ConnectHandler(**device)

        # Run the command to upgrade the firmware
        upgrade_command = f"boot system flash:{firmware_file}"
        connection.send_config_set([upgrade_command])

        # Save the configuration
        connection.send_command("write memory")

        # Reboot the device
        connection.send_command("reload", expect_string="[confirm]")
        connection.send_command("\n", delay_factor=2)
        print(f"Firmware upgrade initiated for {device['host']}.")

        connection.disconnect()
    except Exception as e:
        print(f"Error upgrading firmware on {device['host']}: {e}")
```

```
# Example usage
apply_firmware_upgrade(device, "ios_image.bin")
```

3. Real-World Example: Rolling Out Updates Across a Network

Scenario

You need to upgrade firmware on multiple devices in a network. The firmware image is stored locally and needs to be uploaded and applied to each device.

Complete Automation Script

python

```
from netmiko import ConnectHandler, file_transfer
from datetime import datetime

def backup_config(device, backup_dir):
    try:
        connection = ConnectHandler(**device)
        config = connection.send_command("show running-config")

        timestamp = datetime.now().strftime("%Y%m%d_%H%M%S")
        backup_file = f"{backup_dir}/{device['host']}_config_{timestamp}.txt"
        with open(backup_file, "w") as file:
            file.write(config)
```

```python
        print(f"Configuration backed up for {device['host']} at {backup_file}")
        connection.disconnect()
    except Exception as e:
        print(f"Error backing up configuration for {device['host']}: {e}")


def upload_and_upgrade(device, firmware_file, backup_dir):
    try:
        # Step 1: Backup configuration
        backup_config(device, backup_dir)

        # Step 2: Upload firmware
        print(f"Uploading firmware to {device['host']}...")
        connection = ConnectHandler(**device)
        transfer_result = file_transfer(
            connection,
            source_file=firmware_file,
            dest_file=firmware_file,
            file_system="flash:",
            overwrite_file=True
        )
        if transfer_result["file transferred"]:
            print(f"Firmware uploaded to {device['host']}.")

        # Step 3: Apply the upgrade
        upgrade_command = f"boot system flash:{firmware_file}"
        connection.send_config_set([upgrade_command])
        connection.send_command("write memory")
        connection.send_command("reload", expect_string="[confirm]")
        connection.send_command("\n", delay_factor=2)
```

```
    print(f"Firmware upgrade initiated for {device['host']}.")

    connection.disconnect()
  except Exception as e:
    print(f"Error upgrading firmware on {device['host']}: {e}")


# Define devices and firmware file
devices = [
    {"device_type": "cisco_ios", "host": "192.168.1.1", "username": "admin",
"password": "password"},
    {"device_type": "cisco_ios", "host": "192.168.1.2", "username": "admin",
"password": "password"}
]
firmware_file = "ios_image.bin"
backup_dir = "backups"


# Upgrade devices
for device in devices:
    upload_and_upgrade(device, firmware_file, backup_dir)
```

Output

plaintext

```
Configuration        backed        up        for        192.168.1.1        at
backups/192.168.1.1_config_20250104_150000.txt
Uploading firmware to 192.168.1.1...
Firmware uploaded to 192.168.1.1.
Firmware upgrade initiated for 192.168.1.1.
```

Configuration backed up for 192.168.1.2 at backups/192.168.1.2_config_20250104_150500.txt

Uploading firmware to 192.168.1.2...

Firmware uploaded to 192.168.1.2.

Firmware upgrade initiated for 192.168.1.2.

---

4. Best Practices for Firmware Upgrades

1. **Test in a Lab Environment**:
   - Validate the firmware in a controlled environment before deploying to production.

2. **Backup Configurations**:
   - Always back up running configurations before starting upgrades.

3. **Schedule Downtime**:
   - Perform upgrades during maintenance windows to minimize impact.

4. **Verify Compatibility**:
   - Ensure the firmware is compatible with the device model and existing configurations.

5. **Monitor the Upgrade**:
   - Confirm the device reboots correctly and the firmware is applied.

6. **Automate Logs**:
   - Log backup and upgrade activities for auditing and troubleshooting.

Automating firmware upgrades with Python simplifies the process of maintaining up-to-date network devices. In this chapter, you learned to automate configuration backups, upload firmware, and apply upgrades across multiple devices. These skills are vital for ensuring network security, stability, and performance.

In the next chapter, we'll delve into **Python for Troubleshooting and Diagnostics**, focusing on automating diagnostics to identify and resolve network issues quickly. Let's continue building your network automation expertise!

Chapter 17: Python for Troubleshooting and Diagnostics

Network troubleshooting and diagnostics are vital for identifying and resolving issues that impact performance and reliability. Automating these tasks with Python can significantly enhance efficiency and accuracy. In this chapter, you'll learn how to automate network diagnostics such as **ping**, **traceroute**, and **port scans**. We'll also walk through a real-world example of using Python to identify and isolate network issues.

---

1. Automating Network Diagnostics

Automating Ping Tests
The **ping** command checks connectivity between devices by sending ICMP packets and measuring response time.

Example: Automating Ping with Python

python

import subprocess

def ping_device(ip):

```
try:
    response = subprocess.run(
        ["ping", "-c", "3", ip],
        stdout=subprocess.PIPE,
        stderr=subprocess.PIPE,
        text=True
    )
    if response.returncode == 0:
        print(f"Ping to {ip} successful:\n{response.stdout}")
    else:
        print(f"Ping to {ip} failed:\n{response.stderr}")
except Exception as e:
    print(f"Error pinging {ip}: {e}")

# Example usage
ping_device("192.168.1.1")
```

Automating Traceroute

The **traceroute** command tracks the path packets take to reach a destination, revealing network bottlenecks or failures.

Example: Automating Traceroute

python

```
def traceroute(ip):
    try:
        response = subprocess.run(
            ["traceroute", ip],
            stdout=subprocess.PIPE,
```

```python
        stderr=subprocess.PIPE,
        text=True
    )
    if response.returncode == 0:
        print(f"Traceroute to {ip}:\n{response.stdout}")
    else:
        print(f"Traceroute to {ip} failed:\n{response.stderr}")
  except Exception as e:
    print(f"Error running traceroute to {ip}: {e}")


# Example usage
traceroute("8.8.8.8")
```

Automating Port Scans

Port scanning checks if specific ports on a device are open, indicating available services or potential vulnerabilities.

Example: Automating Port Scans

python

```python
import socket

def scan_ports(ip, ports):
  open_ports = []
  for port in ports:
    with socket.socket(socket.AF_INET, socket.SOCK_STREAM) as s:
      s.settimeout(1)
      result = s.connect_ex((ip, port))
      if result == 0:
```

```
        open_ports.append(port)
    return open_ports


# Example usage
ip = "192.168.1.1"
ports = [22, 80, 443]
open_ports = scan_ports(ip, ports)
print(f"Open ports on {ip}: {open_ports}")
```

2. Real-World Example: Identifying and Isolating Network Issues

Scenario

You need to identify and isolate a network issue causing intermittent connectivity problems between devices. The script will:

1. **Ping** devices to check basic connectivity.
2. Perform a **traceroute** to locate potential bottlenecks.
3. Conduct a **port scan** to ensure critical services are reachable.

Script: Automated Network Diagnostics

python

```
import subprocess
import socket
```

```python
def ping_device(ip):
    print(f"Pinging {ip}...")
    try:
        response = subprocess.run(
            ["ping", "-c", "3", ip],
            stdout=subprocess.PIPE,
            stderr=subprocess.PIPE,
            text=True
        )
        if response.returncode == 0:
            print(f"Ping to {ip} successful.")
            return True
        else:
            print(f"Ping to {ip} failed.")
            return False
    except Exception as e:
        print(f"Error pinging {ip}: {e}")
        return False


def traceroute(ip):
    print(f"Running traceroute to {ip}...")
    try:
        response = subprocess.run(
            ["traceroute", ip],
            stdout=subprocess.PIPE,
            stderr=subprocess.PIPE,
            text=True
        )
        if response.returncode == 0:
            print(f"Traceroute to {ip}:\n{response.stdout}")
```

```
        else:
            print(f"Traceroute to {ip} failed:\n{response.stderr}")
    except Exception as e:
        print(f"Error running traceroute to {ip}: {e}")


def scan_ports(ip, ports):
    print(f"Scanning ports on {ip}...")
    open_ports = []
    for port in ports:
        with socket.socket(socket.AF_INET, socket.SOCK_STREAM) as s:
            s.settimeout(1)
            result = s.connect_ex((ip, port))
            if result == 0:
                open_ports.append(port)
    return open_ports


# Main function for network diagnostics
def diagnose_network(ips, ports):
    for ip in ips:
        print(f"\nDiagnosing {ip}...")
        is_reachable = ping_device(ip)
        if not is_reachable:
            traceroute(ip)
        open_ports = scan_ports(ip, ports)
        print(f"Open ports on {ip}: {open_ports}")


# Example usage
ips = ["192.168.1.1", "8.8.8.8"]
critical_ports = [22, 80, 443]
diagnose_network(ips, critical_ports)
```

Output

plaintext

Diagnosing 192.168.1.1...

Pinging 192.168.1.1...

Ping to 192.168.1.1 successful.

Scanning ports on 192.168.1.1...

Open ports on 192.168.1.1: [22, 80]

Diagnosing 8.8.8.8...

Pinging 8.8.8.8...

Ping to 8.8.8.8 failed.

Running traceroute to 8.8.8.8...

Traceroute to 8.8.8.8:

  1 192.168.0.1 1.2 ms

  2 203.0.113.1 20.3 ms

  ...

Scanning ports on 8.8.8.8...

Open ports on 8.8.8.8: [80, 443]

3. Best Practices for Network Diagnostics Automation

1. **Test Scripts in Controlled Environments**:
    o   Validate scripts in lab environments to prevent unintentional disruptions.
2. **Secure Diagnostic Tools**:

    o Ensure sensitive information (e.g., IPs and credentials) is handled securely.

3. **Log Diagnostic Results**:

    o Save outputs to logs for audit and troubleshooting purposes.

Example:

python

```
with open("diagnostics.log", "a") as logfile:
    logfile.write(response.stdout)
```

4. **Integrate with Monitoring Tools**:

    o Combine diagnostic scripts with tools like Nagios, Zabbix, or SolarWinds for proactive monitoring.

5. **Optimize for Performance**:

    o Limit the frequency of diagnostics to prevent overloading the network.

Python is an invaluable tool for automating network troubleshooting and diagnostics. In this chapter, you learned to automate ping, traceroute, and port scans, culminating in a real-world example of identifying and isolating network issues. These techniques enhance your ability to respond quickly to network problems, minimizing downtime and ensuring smooth operations.

In the next chapter, we'll explore **Automating Network Documentation with Python**, focusing on generating and maintaining up-to-date network documentation automatically. Let's continue building comprehensive network automation solutions!

Chapter 18: Managing IP Address Allocations with Python

Efficient IP address management is essential for maintaining a well-organized and conflict-free network. Automating the assignment, tracking, and verification of IP addresses ensures better resource utilization and reduces administrative overhead. In this chapter, you'll learn how to use Python to automate IP address assignments and conflict checks. We'll also walk through a real-world example of creating an IP Address Management (IPAM) tool.

1. Automating IP Address Assignments and Conflict Checks

Key Concepts in IP Address Management

1. **IP Pool**: A predefined range of IP addresses available for assignment (e.g., 192.168.1.0/24).
2. **Allocation**: Assigning a free IP address from the pool to a device.
3. **Conflict Check**: Ensuring the assigned IP is not already in use or reserved.

4. **Release**: Returning an IP address to the pool when it is no longer in use.

Using Python for IP Address Management

The Python **ipaddress** module provides utilities for managing and validating IP addresses and subnets.

Example: Managing an IP Pool

python

```
import ipaddress

# Define an IP pool
ip_pool = ipaddress.ip_network("192.168.1.0/24")

# Generate a list of available IPs
available_ips = list(ip_pool.hosts())

print(f"Total available IPs: {len(available_ips)}")
print(f"First 5 IPs: {available_ips[:5]}")
```

Automating Conflict Checks

A conflict check verifies that an IP address is not already in use.

Example: Conflict Check

python

```
import os
```

```
def is_ip_in_use(ip):
    response = os.system(f"ping -c 1 {ip} > /dev/null 2>&1")
    return response == 0

# Example usage
ip_to_check = "192.168.1.10"
if is_ip_in_use(ip_to_check):
    print(f"{ip_to_check} is in use.")
else:
    print(f"{ip_to_check} is available.")
```

2. Example: Creating an IP Address Management Tool

Scenario

You need a tool to:

1. Allocate free IP addresses to devices.
2. Check for IP conflicts.
3. Release IP addresses when no longer needed.
4. Store allocations persistently.

Script: IP Address Management Tool
Step 1: Define the IP Pool

python

```
import ipaddress
import json
import os

# Define the IP pool and allocation file
ip_pool = ipaddress.ip_network("192.168.1.0/24")
allocation_file = "ip_allocations.json"

# Initialize allocations
if not os.path.exists(allocation_file):
    with open(allocation_file, "w") as file:
        json.dump({}, file)
```

Step 2: Allocate an IP Address

python

```
def allocate_ip(hostname):
    with open(allocation_file, "r") as file:
        allocations = json.load(file)

    # Find the first available IP
    for ip in ip_pool.hosts():
        if str(ip) not in allocations.values() and not is_ip_in_use(str(ip)):
            allocations[hostname] = str(ip)
            with open(allocation_file, "w") as file:
                json.dump(allocations, file, indent=4)
            print(f"Allocated IP {ip} to {hostname}")
            return str(ip)
```

```python
        print("No available IP addresses.")
    return None
```

Step 3: Release an IP Address

python

```python
def release_ip(hostname):
    with open(allocation_file, "r") as file:
        allocations = json.load(file)

    if hostname in allocations:
        released_ip = allocations.pop(hostname)
        with open(allocation_file, "w") as file:
            json.dump(allocations, file, indent=4)
        print(f"Released IP {released_ip} for {hostname}")
        return released_ip

    print(f"No IP found for {hostname}")
    return None
```

Step 4: Check Allocations

python

```python
def show_allocations():
    with open(allocation_file, "r") as file:
        allocations = json.load(file)
```

```python
    if allocations:
        print("Current IP Allocations:")
        for hostname, ip in allocations.items():
            print(f"{hostname}: {ip}")
    else:
        print("No IP allocations.")
```

Step 5: Main Function

python

```python
def ip_management():
    while True:
        print("\nIP Address Management Tool")
        print("1. Allocate IP")
        print("2. Release IP")
        print("3. Show Allocations")
        print("4. Exit")
        choice = input("Enter your choice: ")

        if choice == "1":
            hostname = input("Enter hostname: ")
            allocate_ip(hostname)
        elif choice == "2":
            hostname = input("Enter hostname: ")
            release_ip(hostname)
        elif choice == "3":
            show_allocations()
        elif choice == "4":
            print("Exiting tool.")
```

```
        break
    else:
        print("Invalid choice. Try again.")


# Run the tool
ip_management()
```

Output

plaintext

IP Address Management Tool

1. Allocate IP

2. Release IP

3. Show Allocations

4. Exit

Enter your choice: 1

Enter hostname: Server1

Allocated IP 192.168.1.1 to Server1

IP Address Management Tool

1. Allocate IP

2. Release IP

3. Show Allocations

4. Exit

Enter your choice: 3

Current IP Allocations:

Server1: 192.168.1.1

IP Address Management Tool

1. Allocate IP

2. Release IP

3. Show Allocations

4. Exit

Enter your choice: 2

Enter hostname: Server1

Released IP 192.168.1.1 for Server1

---

3. Best Practices for IP Address Management

1. **Track Allocations Persistently**:
   - o   Use databases or persistent files (e.g., JSON, CSV) to store allocations.

2. **Conflict Detection**:
   - o   Regularly scan the network to identify unauthorized or duplicate IP assignments.

3. **Integrate with DHCP**:
   - o   Extend scripts to interact with DHCP servers for dynamic IP management.

4. **Reserve Critical IPs**:
   - o   Predefine ranges for critical infrastructure (e.g., routers, firewalls).

5. **Monitor IP Utilization**:
   - o   Generate periodic reports to identify unused or underutilized IPs.

Python simplifies IP address management by automating assignments, conflict checks, and releases. In this chapter, you learned to create an IP Address Management tool, ensuring efficient and conflict-free IP allocations. This tool can be extended to integrate with network monitoring systems and dynamic allocation protocols.

In the next chapter, we'll explore **Automating Network Documentation with Python**, focusing on creating and maintaining comprehensive, up-to-date network documentation automatically. Let's continue building efficient network automation tools!

Chapter 19: Python for Logging and Auditing

Logs are an essential resource for troubleshooting, monitoring, and maintaining a secure network. By automating log collection and analysis, Python can streamline auditing processes, track changes in configurations, and enhance network accountability. This chapter explores how to use Python to automate log collection and analysis, with a real-world example of auditing changes in network configurations.

1. Automating Log Collection and Analysis

Why Automate Log Management?

1. **Centralized Monitoring**:
   o Consolidate logs from multiple devices in a single repository.
2. **Enhanced Security**:
   o Detect suspicious activities or unauthorized changes in real time.
3. **Compliance**:
   o Maintain audit trails for regulatory compliance.

Retrieving Logs via SSH

Python's **Netmiko** library enables you to retrieve logs using CLI commands over SSH.

Example: Fetching Logs from a Cisco Device

python

```python
from netmiko import ConnectHandler

def fetch_logs(device, log_command):
    try:
        print(f"Connecting to {device['host']}...")
        connection = ConnectHandler(**device)

        # Execute the log command
        logs = connection.send_command(log_command)

        # Save logs to a file
        log_file = f"logs/{device['host']}_logs.txt"
        with open(log_file, "w") as file:
            file.write(logs)

        print(f"Logs saved for {device['host']} at {log_file}")
        connection.disconnect()
    except Exception as e:
        print(f"Error fetching logs from {device['host']}: {e}")

# Example usage
```

```
device = {"device_type": "cisco_ios", "host": "192.168.1.1", "username":
"admin", "password": "password"}
fetch_logs(device, "show logging")
```

Parsing Logs for Analysis

Once logs are collected, Python can analyze them for specific patterns or anomalies.

Example: Identifying Errors in Logs

python

```
def parse_logs(log_file, keyword):
    with open(log_file, "r") as file:
        lines = file.readlines()

    matched_lines = [line for line in lines if keyword in line]
    return matched_lines

# Example usage
error_logs = parse_logs("logs/192.168.1.1_logs.txt", "ERROR")
print("Error Logs:")
for log in error_logs:
    print(log.strip())
```

2. Real-World Example: Auditing Changes in Network Configurations

Scenario

You need to monitor and audit changes in network device configurations to:

1. Track unauthorized modifications.
2. Maintain a history of configuration states for troubleshooting.
3. Generate audit reports for compliance purposes.

Steps for Configuration Auditing

Step 1: Collect Running Configurations Retrieve the current running configuration from each device and save it locally.

Step 2: Compare Configurations Compare the current configuration with a previously saved baseline to identify changes.

Step 3: Log and Report Changes Generate a report highlighting any differences.

Script: Configuration Auditing

python

```
from netmiko import ConnectHandler
from difflib import unified_diff
from datetime import datetime
```

```
import os

# Directory for storing configuration files
config_dir = "config_backups"
os.makedirs(config_dir, exist_ok=True)

def fetch_config(device):
    try:
        print(f"Fetching configuration from {device['host']}...")
        connection = ConnectHandler(**device)
        config = connection.send_command("show running-config")
        connection.disconnect()

        # Save the current configuration
        timestamp = datetime.now().strftime("%Y%m%d_%H%M%S")
        config_file = f"{config_dir}/{device['host']}_config_{timestamp}.txt"
        with open(config_file, "w") as file:
            file.write(config)
        print(f"Configuration saved at {config_file}")
        return config_file
    except Exception as e:
        print(f"Error fetching configuration from {device['host']}: {e}")
        return None

def compare_configs(old_file, new_file):
    with open(old_file, "r") as old, open(new_file, "r") as new:
        old_config = old.readlines()
        new_config = new.readlines()
```

```python
    diff = unified_diff(old_config, new_config, fromfile="Baseline",
tofile="Current", lineterm="")
    return list(diff)


def audit_config_changes(device):
    # Fetch the current configuration
    current_config_file = fetch_config(device)

    # Get the latest saved configuration for comparison
    previous_files = sorted(
        [f for f in os.listdir(config_dir) if f.startswith(device['host'])],
        reverse=True
    )
    if len(previous_files) > 1:
        baseline_file = f"{config_dir}/{previous_files[1]}"
        print(f"Comparing {baseline_file} with {current_config_file}...")
        changes = compare_configs(baseline_file, current_config_file)

        if changes:
            print("Configuration changes detected:")
            for line in changes:
                print(line)
        else:
            print("No changes detected.")
    else:
        print("No baseline configuration available for comparison.")


# Example usage
device = {"device_type": "cisco_ios", "host": "192.168.1.1", "username":
"admin", "password": "password"}
```

audit_config_changes(device)

Output

plaintext

Fetching configuration from 192.168.1.1...

Configuration   saved   at config_backups/192.168.1.1_config_20250104_153000.txt

Comparing   config_backups/192.168.1.1_config_20250104_150000.txt   with config_backups/192.168.1.1_config_20250104_153000.txt...

Configuration changes detected:

--- Baseline

+++ Current

@@ -12,7 +12,7 @@

 interface GigabitEthernet0/1

 description Old Description

 ip address 192.168.1.1 255.255.255.0

- no shutdown

+ shutdown

!

---

3. Best Practices for Logging and Auditing

1. **Centralize Log Storage**:

    o   Use centralized systems like Elastic Stack or Graylog for storing and analyzing logs.

2. **Encrypt Logs**:

- o Secure sensitive logs with encryption to prevent unauthorized access.

3. **Automate Baseline Comparisons**:
   - o Schedule regular comparisons between current configurations and baselines.

4. **Set Alerts**:
   - o Configure alerts for specific log patterns, such as unauthorized changes or critical errors.

5. **Maintain Logs for Compliance**:
   - o Store logs and configuration snapshots for an extended period to meet compliance requirements.

Python simplifies logging and auditing by automating log collection, analysis, and configuration comparisons. In this chapter, you learned to retrieve logs, parse and analyze them, and implement a real-world example of auditing configuration changes. These tools enhance your ability to monitor and maintain secure and compliant network operations.

In the next chapter, we'll explore **Python for Network Visualization**, focusing on creating interactive network topology maps and performance dashboards. Let's continue building robust network management solutions!

Chapter 20: Integrating Python with SDN and NFV

Software-Defined Networking (SDN) and Network Function Virtualization (NFV) are revolutionizing network architecture by enabling centralized control, flexibility, and scalability. Python plays a crucial role in automating SDN and NFV tasks, integrating with controllers, and implementing dynamic network functionalities. In this chapter, you'll learn about SDN and NFV, explore Python's integration with tools like OpenFlow and OpenDaylight, and implement a real-world example of automating path selection in SDN environments.

---

1. Understanding SDN and NFV

What is SDN?

- **Software-Defined Networking (SDN)** decouples the control plane (decision-making) from the data plane (packet forwarding).
- **Key Components**:
  - **SDN Controller**: Centralized management, such as OpenDaylight or ONOS.

o **Data Plane**: Network devices like switches and routers.

o **Northbound APIs**: Interface for applications to communicate with the controller.

o **Southbound APIs**: Interface for the controller to communicate with devices (e.g., OpenFlow).

What is NFV?

- **Network Function Virtualization (NFV)** replaces dedicated hardware appliances (e.g., firewalls, load balancers) with virtualized network functions (VNFs) running on standard servers.

Benefits of SDN and NFV

1. **Centralized Control**:
   o Simplifies network management and improves visibility.
2. **Dynamic Resource Allocation**:
   o Adapts to changing demands in real time.
3. **Cost Efficiency**:
   o Reduces dependency on specialized hardware.

2. Using Python with OpenFlow and OpenDaylight

OpenFlow

- OpenFlow is a protocol that allows an SDN controller to communicate with switches.
- Python libraries like **Ryu** enable OpenFlow-based development.

Example: Installing an OpenFlow Rule

python

```
from ryu.base import app_manager
from ryu.controller import ofp_event
from ryu.controller.handler import CONFIG_DISPATCHER, MAIN_DISPATCHER
from ryu.controller.handler import set_ev_cls
from ryu.ofproto import ofproto_v1_3

class SimpleSwitch(app_manager.RyuApp):
    OFP_VERSIONS = [ofproto_v1_3.OFP_VERSION]

    def __init__(self, *args, **kwargs):
        super(SimpleSwitch, self).__init__(*args, **kwargs)

    @set_ev_cls(ofp_event.EventOFPSwitchFeatures, CONFIG_DISPATCHER)
    def switch_features_handler(self, ev):
        datapath = ev.msg.datapath
        ofproto = datapath.ofproto
        parser = datapath.ofproto_parser
```

```python
    # Match all packets and send to controller
    match = parser.OFPMatch()
    actions = [parser.OFPActionOutput(ofproto.OFPP_CONTROLLER)]
    self.add_flow(datapath, 0, match, actions)

  def add_flow(self, datapath, priority, match, actions):
    ofproto = datapath.ofproto
    parser = datapath.ofproto_parser
    instructions                                                =
[parser.OFPInstructionActions(ofproto.OFPIT_APPLY_ACTIONS, actions)]
    mod = parser.OFPFlowMod(
      datapath=datapath,          priority=priority,          match=match,
instructions=instructions
    )
    datapath.send_msg(mod)
```

OpenDaylight

OpenDaylight is an SDN controller with REST APIs for managing network devices.

Example: Using Python with OpenDaylight

python

```python
import requests
from requests.auth import HTTPBasicAuth

# OpenDaylight API configuration
url    =    "http://localhost:8181/restconf/operational/network-topology:network-topology"
```

```
auth = HTTPBasicAuth("admin", "admin")

# Fetch network topology
response = requests.get(url, auth=auth)
if response.status_code == 200:
    topology = response.json()
    print("Network Topology:", topology)
else:
    print(f"Failed to fetch topology: {response.status_code}")
```

3. Real-World Example: Automating Path Selection in SDN Environments

Scenario

In an SDN environment, you need to dynamically select and configure the optimal path between hosts based on bandwidth availability and latency.

Steps for Path Selection Automation

1. **Fetch Network Topology**:
   o Retrieve the current topology from the SDN controller.
2. **Evaluate Path Metrics**:
   o Calculate bandwidth and latency for available paths.
3. **Install Flow Rules**:

o   Configure switches along the selected path.

Script: Path Selection Automation

python

```python
import requests
from requests.auth import HTTPBasicAuth

# OpenDaylight API configuration
controller_url = "http://localhost:8181/restconf"
auth = HTTPBasicAuth("admin", "admin")

def fetch_topology():
    url = f"{controller_url}/operational/network-topology:network-topology"
    response = requests.get(url, auth=auth)
    if response.status_code == 200:
        return response.json()
    else:
        print(f"Failed to fetch topology: {response.status_code}")
        return None

def calculate_optimal_path(topology, src, dst):
    # Placeholder for path calculation logic
    # Example: Find the shortest path using latency or bandwidth
    paths = topology["network-topology"]["topology"][0]["link"]
    optimal_path = paths[0]  # Example: Select the first path
    return optimal_path
```

```
def install_flow_rule(src, dst, path):
    # Placeholder for installing flow rules
    print(f"Installing flow from {src} to {dst} via {path}")


# Main function
def automate_path_selection(src, dst):
    topology = fetch_topology()
    if topology:
        optimal_path = calculate_optimal_path(topology, src, dst)
        if optimal_path:
            install_flow_rule(src, dst, optimal_path)
        else:
            print("No optimal path found.")


# Example usage
src_host = "10.0.0.1"
dst_host = "10.0.0.2"
automate_path_selection(src_host, dst_host)
```

Output

plaintext

Fetching network topology...
Installing flow from 10.0.0.1 to 10.0.0.2 via link1

4. Best Practices for Python Integration with SDN and NFV

1. **Secure API Communications**:

   o   Use HTTPS and authentication tokens to secure API calls.

2. **Test in Lab Environments**:

   o   Validate automation scripts in a controlled environment before deploying to production.

3. **Monitor Controller Performance**:

   o   Ensure that frequent API calls do not overload the SDN controller.

4. **Leverage Path Optimization Algorithms**:

   o   Use advanced algorithms like Dijkstra or Bellman-Ford for efficient path selection.

5. **Integrate with NFV Orchestrators**:

   o   Extend automation scripts to manage VNFs using orchestration platforms like OpenStack.

Python provides powerful capabilities for automating and managing SDN and NFV environments. In this chapter, you learned to interact with OpenFlow and OpenDaylight, culminating in a real-world example of automating path selection in an SDN environment. These techniques enhance your ability to manage dynamic, scalable, and efficient networks.

In the next chapter, we'll delve into **Python for Network Visualization**, focusing on creating interactive topology maps and performance dashboards. Let's continue building advanced network automation solutions!

Chapter 21: Working with Network Simulation Tools

Network simulation tools such as **GNS3**, **Cisco VIRL**, and **EVE-NG** are essential for testing and validating network configurations before deploying them in production. Python can enhance the capabilities of these tools by automating repetitive tasks, deploying topologies, and running simulation scenarios. This chapter explores using Python with these tools, automating network simulations, and provides a real-world example of deploying topologies in GNS3.

1. Using Python with GNS3, Cisco VIRL, and EVE-NG

GNS3

- **Graphical Network Simulator** used for simulating complex networks.
- Python integration via the **GNS3 API** allows you to automate actions such as deploying nodes and managing connections.

GNS3 API Example:

bash

http://<gns3_server>:3080/v2

Cisco VIRL

- Cisco's **Virtual Internet Routing Lab** for simulating Cisco network topologies.
- Python integration via **Cisco VIRL APIs** to automate simulations.

Cisco VIRL API Example:

bash

http://<virl_server>:8888/api

EVE-NG

- **Emulated Virtual Environment-Next Generation** supports multi-vendor network simulations.
- Python integration via the **EVE-NG API** for deploying and managing labs.

EVE-NG API Example:

bash

https://<eve_ng_server>/api

2. Automating Network Simulation Scenarios

Key Steps in Automation

1. **Define Topology**:
   o Specify nodes, connections, and configurations.
2. **Deploy Nodes**:
   o Use APIs to create devices in the simulation environment.
3. **Establish Connections**:
   o Automate link creation between devices.
4. **Run and Monitor Simulations**:
   o Start devices and collect metrics or logs for analysis.

Example: Automating a Topology in GNS3
Prerequisites:

- Install GNS3 Server and ensure the API is enabled.
- Install the requests library:

bash

```
pip install requests
```

Step 1: Define the Topology

python

```python
import requests

gns3_server = "http://localhost:3080/v2"
project_name = "SampleTopology"

# Create a new project
def create_project(project_name):
    url = f"{gns3_server}/projects"
    response = requests.post(url, json={"name": project_name})
    if response.status_code == 201:
        project_id = response.json()["project_id"]
        print(f"Project '{project_name}' created with ID: {project_id}")
        return project_id
    else:
        print(f"Failed to create project: {response.text}")
        return None
```

Step 2: Add Nodes to the Project

python

```python
def add_node(project_id, node_name, template):
    url = f"{gns3_server}/projects/{project_id}/nodes"
    payload = {
        "name": node_name,
        "node_type": "qemu",
        "template_id": template  # Replace with your GNS3 template ID
    }
```

```
response = requests.post(url, json=payload)
if response.status_code == 201:
    node_id = response.json()["node_id"]
    print(f"Node '{node_name}' added with ID: {node_id}")
    return node_id
else:
    print(f"Failed to add node: {response.text}")
    return None
```

Step 3: Connect Nodes

python

```
def connect_nodes(project_id, node1_id, node2_id):
    url = f"{gns3_server}/projects/{project_id}/links"
    payload = {
        "nodes": [
            {"node_id": node1_id, "adapter_number": 0, "port_number": 0},
            {"node_id": node2_id, "adapter_number": 0, "port_number": 1}
        ]
    }
    response = requests.post(url, json=payload)
    if response.status_code == 201:
        print("Nodes connected successfully.")
    else:
        print(f"Failed to connect nodes: {response.text}")
```

Step 4: Automate the Workflow

python

```python
def automate_topology():
    project_id = create_project(project_name)
    if project_id:
        router1_id = add_node(project_id, "Router1", "router_template_id")
        router2_id = add_node(project_id, "Router2", "router_template_id")
        if router1_id and router2_id:
            connect_nodes(project_id, router1_id, router2_id)
            print("Topology deployed successfully.")
        else:
            print("Failed to add nodes.")
    else:
        print("Failed to create project.")

# Run the automation
automate_topology()
```

Output

plaintext

Project 'SampleTopology' created with ID: 12345

Node 'Router1' added with ID: abcde

Node 'Router2' added with ID: fghij

Nodes connected successfully.

Topology deployed successfully.

3. Best Practices for Automating Simulations

1. **Validate Topology Design**:
   - o Ensure the defined topology meets simulation objectives before deployment.

2. **Use Templates**:
   - o Predefine templates for devices to simplify automation.

3. **Log Automation Actions**:
   - o Maintain logs for API requests and responses to troubleshoot errors.

4. **Secure API Access**:
   - o Use secure communication (e.g., HTTPS) and authenticate API calls.

5. **Monitor Simulation Performance**:
   - o Ensure that simulations do not overload the server or compromise performance.

Python simplifies the management of network simulation tools like GNS3, Cisco VIRL, and EVE-NG by automating tasks such as topology deployment and scenario execution. In this chapter, you learned to integrate Python with these tools, automate simulation scenarios, and create a real-world script for deploying topologies in

GNS3. These techniques allow you to efficiently test and validate network configurations in a controlled environment.

In the next chapter, we'll explore **Python for Network Visualization**, focusing on creating interactive topology maps and performance dashboards. Let's continue building advanced network automation solutions!

Chapter 22: Building Network Dashboards

Network dashboards are essential for providing a centralized view of real-time metrics, visualizing performance, and simplifying network management. Python frameworks like **Flask** and **Dash** enable the creation of interactive, web-based dashboards to monitor and analyze network data. In this chapter, you'll learn to use these frameworks to build dashboards, display real-time metrics, and create a real-world network performance dashboard.

1. Using Python Frameworks to Build Dashboards

Flask

- Flask is a lightweight web framework for building APIs and dynamic web applications.
- Ideal for integrating data collection and display.

Basic Flask Example:

python

from flask import Flask

```python
app = Flask(__name__)

@app.route("/")
def home():
    return "Welcome to the Network Dashboard"

if __name__ == "__main__":
    app.run(debug=True)
```

Dash

- Dash is a Python framework for creating interactive dashboards with data visualizations.
- Built on Flask, Plotly, and React.js.
- Provides powerful tools for creating real-time, interactive components.

Basic Dash Example:

python

```python
from dash import Dash, html

app = Dash(__name__)

app.layout = html.Div(children=[
    html.H1("Network Dashboard"),
    html.P("Real-time network metrics will appear here.")
```

```
])

if __name__ == "__main__":
    app.run_server(debug=True)
```

---

2. Displaying Real-Time Network Metrics in Dashboards

Key Metrics to Display

1. **Latency**: Round-trip time for packets.
2. **Bandwidth**: Data transfer rate.
3. **Uptime**: Duration of device or link availability.
4. **Device Status**: Online/offline status of devices.

Collecting Real-Time Metrics

Real-time metrics can be collected using tools like **ping**, **SNMP**, or API integrations with network monitoring tools.

Example: Fetching Latency Data

python

```
import subprocess

def get_latency(ip):
    try:
        response = subprocess.run(
            ["ping", "-c", "1", ip],
            stdout=subprocess.PIPE,
```

```
        stderr=subprocess.PIPE,
        text=True
    )
    if response.returncode == 0:
        latency_line = [line for line in response.stdout.split("\n") if "time=" in
line]
        latency = latency_line[0].split("time=")[-1].split(" ")[0]
        return float(latency)
    return None
  except Exception as e:
    print(f"Error fetching latency for {ip}: {e}")
    return None
```

3. Real-World Example: Creating a Network Performance Dashboard

Scenario

Build a dashboard to monitor:

1. Latency to critical devices.
2. Bandwidth utilization.
3. Device status (online/offline).

Step 1: Collect Metrics

Write a script to fetch metrics from the network.

python

```
import os

def check_device_status(ip):
    response = os.system(f"ping -c 1 {ip} > /dev/null 2>&1")
    return "Online" if response == 0 else "Offline"

# Example usage
devices = ["192.168.1.1", "8.8.8.8"]
status = {ip: check_device_status(ip) for ip in devices}
print(status)
```

Step 2: Build the Dashboard

Use Dash to display the metrics.

python

```
from dash import Dash, dcc, html
from dash.dependencies import Input, Output
import time

app = Dash(__name__)

# Sample devices
devices = ["192.168.1.1", "8.8.8.8"]

# Function to simulate real-time metrics
def fetch_metrics():
    return [
        {"device": ip, "status": check_device_status(ip), "latency": get_latency(ip)}
```

```python
        for ip in devices
    ]


app.layout = html.Div([
    html.H1("Network Performance Dashboard"),
    html.Div(id="live-metrics"),
    dcc.Interval(
        id="interval-component",
        interval=5000,  # Refresh every 5 seconds
        n_intervals=0
    )
])


@app.callback(
    Output("live-metrics", "children"),
    [Input("interval-component", "n_intervals")]
)
def update_metrics(n):
    metrics = fetch_metrics()
    return [
        html.Div([
            html.P(f"Device: {m['device']}"),
            html.P(f"Status: {m['status']}"),
            html.P(f"Latency: {m['latency']} ms")
        ]) for m in metrics
    ]


if __name__ == "__main__":
    app.run_server(debug=True)
```

Step 3: Visualize Metrics

Enhance the dashboard with graphs using **Plotly**.

Adding a Latency Graph:

python

```python
import plotly.graph_objs as go

latency_data = []

@app.callback(
    Output("live-metrics", "children"),
    Output("latency-graph", "figure"),
    [Input("interval-component", "n_intervals")]
)
def update_metrics_and_graph(n):
    metrics = fetch_metrics()
    latency_data.append({
        "time": time.time(),
        "latencies": [m["latency"] for m in metrics]
    })

    fig = go.Figure()
    for i, device in enumerate(devices):
        fig.add_trace(go.Scatter(
            x=[d["time"] for d in latency_data],
            y=[d["latencies"][i] for d in latency_data],
            mode="lines",
            name=f"Latency: {device}"
        ))
```

```
return [
  html.Div([
    html.P(f"Device: {m['device']}"),
    html.P(f"Status: {m['status']}"),
    html.P(f"Latency: {m['latency']} ms")
  ]) for m in metrics
], fig


app.layout = html.Div([
  html.H1("Network Performance Dashboard"),
  html.Div(id="live-metrics"),
  dcc.Graph(id="latency-graph"),
  dcc.Interval(
    id="interval-component",
    interval=5000,
    n_intervals=0
  )
])
```

4. Best Practices for Building Network Dashboards

1. **Real-Time Updates**:
   - Use intervals to refresh metrics dynamically.

2. **Scalability**:
   - Optimize data collection scripts to handle large networks.

3. **Interactive Elements**:

o Add filtering, sorting, and device selection options.

4. **Secure Access**:

   o Authenticate users before granting access to the dashboard.

5. **Extend with APIs**:

   o Integrate with APIs from monitoring tools like SolarWinds or Zabbix for enriched data.

Building network dashboards with Python enables centralized, real-time monitoring of critical metrics. In this chapter, you learned to use Flask and Dash to create web-based dashboards, collect and display real-time network data, and build a network performance dashboard. These tools provide actionable insights, simplify management, and enhance network reliability.

In the next chapter, we'll explore **Python for Custom Network Tools**, focusing on developing tailored solutions to address specific network challenges. Let's continue building advanced network automation solutions!

Chapter 23: Python for Zero-Touch Provisioning (ZTP)

Zero-Touch Provisioning (ZTP) simplifies the onboarding of network devices by automating initial configuration and deployment tasks. With Python, ZTP workflows can be customized to efficiently onboard devices without manual intervention, reducing time and operational costs. This chapter explores how to use Python to automate device onboarding and includes a real-world example of deploying switches with ZTP.

---

1. Automating Device Onboarding with Python

What is Zero-Touch Provisioning (ZTP)?

ZTP is a process where a new network device:

1. Automatically requests its initial configuration upon boot.
2. Fetches necessary files (e.g., configuration, firmware) from a central server.
3. Applies the configuration and becomes operational.

Why Use Python for ZTP?

1. **Flexibility**:
   o Customize workflows for different device types and environments.
2. **Scalability**:
   o Onboard multiple devices simultaneously.
3. **Integration**:
   o Leverage APIs, DHCP, TFTP, and other services to streamline provisioning.

Key Steps in ZTP Workflow

1. **Device Boot**:
   o Device boots and requests an IP address via DHCP.
2. **Script Invocation**:
   o The DHCP server points the device to a Python script or configuration file.
3. **Configuration Fetch**:
   o Python retrieves configurations and firmware via protocols like TFTP or HTTP.
4. **Apply Configuration**:
   o The device applies the fetched configuration.

---

2. Real-World Example: Zero-Touch Switch Deployment

Scenario

Deploy a new switch into a network:

1. Assign an IP address via DHCP.
2. Fetch an initial configuration file from a central server.
3. Apply the configuration and verify connectivity.

Step 1: Set Up a Central Server

Ensure the server has:

1. **DHCP Service**:
   - Assigns IP addresses to devices and points them to the ZTP script.
2. **Python Environment**:
   - Executes the ZTP logic.
3. **File Transfer Service**:
   - Provides configuration files (e.g., via TFTP, FTP, or HTTP).

Step 2: Write the ZTP Script

Script for Zero-Touch Deployment:

```python
python

import os
```

```python
import time
from ftplib import FTP

# Define device-specific configurations
CONFIG_DIR = "/ztp/configs/"
LOG_FILE = "/ztp/logs/ztp.log"

def log_message(message):
    """Log ZTP activities."""
    with open(LOG_FILE, "a") as log:
        log.write(f"{time.strftime('%Y-%m-%d %H:%M:%S')} - {message}\n")
    print(message)

def fetch_config(device_id, server_ip):
    """Fetch the configuration file for the device."""
    config_file = f"{CONFIG_DIR}{device_id}.cfg"
    try:
        ftp = FTP(server_ip)
        ftp.login()
        with open(config_file, "wb") as local_file:
            ftp.retrbinary(f"RETR {device_id}.cfg", local_file.write)
        ftp.quit()
        log_message(f"Configuration fetched for device {device_id}")
        return config_file
    except Exception as e:
        log_message(f"Error fetching configuration for {device_id}: {e}")
        return None

def apply_config(device_ip, config_file):
    """Simulate applying configuration to the device."""
```

```python
    try:
        # Example: Using SSH to push configuration
        os.system(f"ssh admin@{device_ip} < {config_file}")
        log_message(f"Configuration applied to device {device_ip}")
        return True
    except Exception as e:
        log_message(f"Error applying configuration to {device_ip}: {e}")
        return False


def ztp_process(device_id, device_ip, server_ip):
    """Complete ZTP process for a device."""
    log_message(f"Starting ZTP process for device {device_id} ({device_ip})")

    # Step 1: Fetch configuration
    config_file = fetch_config(device_id, server_ip)
    if not config_file:
        log_message(f"ZTP process failed for {device_id}")
        return False

    # Step 2: Apply configuration
    if apply_config(device_ip, config_file):
        log_message(f"ZTP process completed successfully for {device_id}")
        return True
    else:
        log_message(f"ZTP process failed for {device_id}")
        return False

# Example usage
device_id = "switch01"
device_ip = "192.168.1.100"
```

```
server_ip = "192.168.1.1"
ztp_process(device_id, device_ip, server_ip)
```

Step 3: DHCP Configuration

Configure the DHCP server to point new devices to the ZTP script.

Example DHCP Configuration:

plaintext

```
subnet 192.168.1.0 netmask 255.255.255.0 {
    range 192.168.1.100 192.168.1.200;
    option tftp-server-name "192.168.1.1";
    option bootfile-name "ztp_script.py";
}
```

Step 4: Provide Device Configuration Files

Store individual configuration files (e.g., switch01.cfg, switch02.cfg) on the server in the /ztp/configs/ directory.

Example Configuration File (switch01.cfg):

plaintext

```
hostname Switch01
interface GigabitEthernet0/1
 description Uplink
 ip address 192.168.1.100 255.255.255.0
 no shutdown
```

!

Step 5: Automate Logging and Alerts

Track ZTP activities and send alerts for failures.

Add Logging:

python

log_message("ZTP process started for all devices")

Send Alerts: Integrate with an email or messaging API (e.g., SMTP, Slack) to notify administrators of failures.

---

3. Best Practices for ZTP

1. **Use Unique Device Identifiers**:
   - o Base configurations on device MAC addresses or serial numbers for uniqueness.
2. **Secure File Transfers**:
   - o Use secure protocols (e.g., SFTP or HTTPS) to transfer configurations.
3. **Test in a Lab Environment**:
   - o Validate ZTP scripts with a variety of device types and configurations.
4. **Version Control for Configurations**:

- ○ Store configuration files in a version control system like Git for easy tracking.

5. **Monitor ZTP Progress**:

   - ○ Implement logging and real-time monitoring to identify and resolve issues quickly.

Zero-Touch Provisioning (ZTP) automates the tedious task of onboarding network devices, improving efficiency and reducing errors. In this chapter, you learned to use Python to implement a ZTP workflow, fetch configurations, apply them to devices, and monitor the process. These tools are invaluable for scaling network deployments and ensuring consistent configurations.

In the next chapter, we'll explore **Python for Custom Network Tools**, focusing on developing tailored solutions for unique network challenges. Let's continue building advanced network automation capabilities!

Chapter 24: Handling Multi-Vendor Networks

Managing multi-vendor networks introduces complexity due to differences in device configurations, command-line interfaces, and APIs. Python offers powerful tools to unify workflows and automate tasks across diverse network environments. In this chapter, we'll explore the challenges of managing multi-vendor networks, learn to write Python scripts for unified workflows, and implement a real-world example of automating configurations for Cisco, Juniper, and Arista devices.

---

1. Challenges of Multi-Vendor Environments

1.1 Inconsistent Command Syntax

- Different vendors use unique commands for the same tasks.
    - **Example**: Setting an interface description:
        - Cisco: description
        - Juniper: set description
        - Arista: description

1.2 Varied Management Protocols

- Some devices rely on CLI over SSH, while others offer REST APIs or NETCONF/YANG for configuration.

1.3 Lack of Standardized Configurations

- Applying consistent configurations across multiple vendors requires converting templates to each vendor's syntax.

1.4 Compatibility and Integration Issues

- Tools and scripts must accommodate vendor-specific quirks and limitations.

---

2. Writing Python Scripts to Unify Workflows

Using Python Libraries for Multi-Vendor Automation

1. **Netmiko**:
   o A CLI-based library supporting multiple vendors.
2. **NAPALM**:
   o Abstracts differences by offering a consistent API for interacting with various devices.
3. **Paramiko**:
   o Enables direct SSH connections for custom scripts.
4. **PyEZ** (Juniper):

o A library for automating Juniper devices using NETCONF.

5. **EAPI** (Arista):

o Allows interaction with Arista devices using REST or JSON-RPC APIs.

Unified Workflow with Netmiko

Netmiko simplifies automation by providing device-specific drivers for vendors.

Example: Sending Unified Commands to Multi-Vendor Devices

python

```
from netmiko import ConnectHandler

# Define device configurations
devices = [
    {"device_type": "cisco_ios", "host": "192.168.1.1", "username": "admin",
"password": "password"},
    {"device_type": "juniper", "host": "192.168.1.2", "username": "admin",
"password": "password"},
    {"device_type": "arista_eos", "host": "192.168.1.3", "username": "admin",
"password": "password"}
]

# Define a function to send a command
def send_command_to_device(device, command):
```

```python
    try:
        connection = ConnectHandler(**device)
        output = connection.send_command(command)
        print(f"Output from {device['host']}:\n{output}")
        connection.disconnect()
    except Exception as e:
        print(f"Error connecting to {device['host']}: {e}")


# Example usage
command = "show version"
for device in devices:
    send_command_to_device(device, command)
```

Unified Configuration with NAPALM

NAPALM abstracts vendor differences by providing a consistent API for configuration management.

Example: Configuring Interfaces with NAPALM

python

```python
from napalm import get_network_driver

def configure_interface(device, interface, description):
    driver = get_network_driver(device["vendor"])
    with driver(hostname=device["host"], username=device["username"],
password=device["password"]) as conn:
        conn.load_merge_candidate(config=f"interface {interface}\n description
{description}\n")
        diff = conn.compare_config()
```

```
    if diff:
      print(f"Changes for {device['host']}:\n{diff}")
      conn.commit_config()
    else:
      print(f"No changes required for {device['host']}.")
```

```
# Example usage
devices = [
  {"vendor": "ios", "host": "192.168.1.1", "username": "admin", "password":
"password"},
  {"vendor": "junos", "host": "192.168.1.2", "username": "admin", "password":
"password"},
  {"vendor": "eos", "host": "192.168.1.3", "username": "admin", "password":
"password"}
]
```

```
for device in devices:
  configure_interface(device, "GigabitEthernet0/1", "Connected to core switch")
```

3. Real-World Example: Automating Configurations for Cisco, Juniper, and Arista Devices

Scenario

You need to apply a consistent VLAN configuration across switches from Cisco, Juniper, and Arista.

Unified VLAN Configuration Script

236

```python
python

from netmiko import ConnectHandler

# Define devices
devices = [
    {"device_type": "cisco_ios", "host": "192.168.1.1", "username": "admin", "password": "password"},
    {"device_type": "juniper", "host": "192.168.1.2", "username": "admin", "password": "password"},
    {"device_type": "arista_eos", "host": "192.168.1.3", "username": "admin", "password": "password"}
]

# Define VLAN configuration templates
vlan_configs = {
    "cisco_ios": [
        "vlan 10",
        "name Employees",
        "vlan 20",
        "name Guests"
    ],
    "juniper": [
        "set vlans VLAN10 vlan-id 10",
        "set vlans VLAN10 description Employees",
        "set vlans VLAN20 vlan-id 20",
        "set vlans VLAN20 description Guests"
    ],
    "arista_eos": [
        "vlan 10",
```

```
        "name Employees",
        "vlan 20",
        "name Guests"
    ]
}


# Apply configuration
def apply_vlan_config(device):
    try:
        connection = ConnectHandler(**device)
        device_type = device["device_type"]
        commands = vlan_configs.get(device_type, [])
        if commands:
            connection.send_config_set(commands)
            print(f"VLAN configuration applied to {device['host']}")
        else:
            print(f"No    VLAN    configuration    available    for    {device['host']}
({device_type})")
        connection.disconnect()
    except Exception as e:
        print(f"Error configuring {device['host']}: {e}")


# Execute configuration for all devices
for device in devices:
    apply_vlan_config(device)
```

Output

plaintext

VLAN configuration applied to 192.168.1.1

VLAN configuration applied to 192.168.1.2

VLAN configuration applied to 192.168.1.3

4. Best Practices for Multi-Vendor Automation

1. **Abstract Vendor-Specific Logic**:
   o Use libraries like NAPALM or create vendor-specific configuration templates.

2. **Use Modular Scripts**:
   o Write reusable functions for tasks like authentication, command execution, and logging.

3. **Test Configurations in Lab Environments**:
   o Validate scripts on lab devices before deploying them in production.

4. **Document Differences**:
   o Maintain a reference for vendor-specific command syntax and quirks.

5. **Secure Automation**:
   o Encrypt sensitive information like credentials and use secure APIs where possible.

Managing multi-vendor networks is challenging, but Python provides tools to unify workflows and streamline configuration management. In this chapter, you learned to address multi-vendor challenges, write unified Python scripts, and implement a real-world example of automating VLAN configurations across Cisco, Juniper, and Arista devices. These techniques enhance operational efficiency and ensure consistency in diverse network environments.

In the next chapter, we'll explore **Python for Network Security**, focusing on automating tasks like access control management and intrusion detection. Let's continue building advanced network automation solutions!

Chapter 25: Real-World Case Studies in Python Network Automation

---

This chapter explores three real-world case studies that highlight the transformative power of Python in network automation. These examples demonstrate how Python can solve specific challenges, streamline workflows, and enhance operational efficiency in diverse network environments.

Case Study 1: Automating a Network Upgrade in an Enterprise Environment

Scenario

An enterprise network requires a firmware upgrade across 50 Cisco devices to address security vulnerabilities. The task involves:

1. Backing up current configurations.
2. Uploading new firmware images.
3. Applying the upgrades and verifying success.

Solution

Python automates the entire upgrade process, reducing manual intervention and minimizing downtime.

Implementation:

python

```python
from netmiko import ConnectHandler, file_transfer

def backup_configuration(device):
    try:
        print(f"Backing up configuration for {device['host']}...")
        connection = ConnectHandler(**device)
        config = connection.send_command("show running-config")
        backup_file = f"backups/{device['host']}_backup.txt"
        with open(backup_file, "w") as file:
            file.write(config)
        connection.disconnect()
        print(f"Backup completed for {device['host']}.")
    except Exception as e:
        print(f"Error backing up {device['host']}: {e}")

def upload_firmware(device, firmware):
    try:
        print(f"Uploading firmware to {device['host']}...")
        connection = ConnectHandler(**device)
        transfer_result = file_transfer(
            connection,
            source_file=firmware,
            dest_file=firmware,
            file_system="flash:",
```

```
            overwrite_file=True
        )
        connection.disconnect()
        if transfer_result["file_transferred"]:
            print(f"Firmware uploaded successfully to {device['host']}.")
            return True
        else:
            print(f"Firmware upload failed on {device['host']}.")
            return False
    except Exception as e:
        print(f"Error uploading firmware to {device['host']}: {e}")
        return False


def apply_firmware(device, firmware):
    try:
        print(f"Applying firmware on {device['host']}...")
        connection = ConnectHandler(**device)
        connection.send_config_set([f"boot system flash:{firmware}"])
        connection.send_command("write memory")
        connection.send_command("reload", expect_string="[confirm]")
        connection.send_command("\n", delay_factor=2)
        print(f"Firmware applied on {device['host']}.")
        connection.disconnect()
    except Exception as e:
        print(f"Error applying firmware on {device['host']}: {e}")


# Define devices and firmware
devices = [{"device_type": "cisco_ios", "host": f"192.168.1.{i}", "username":
"admin", "password": "password"} for i in range(1, 51)]
firmware = "ios_upgrade.bin"
```

```
# Automate the upgrade
for device in devices:
  backup_configuration(device)
  if upload_firmware(device, firmware):
    apply_firmware(device, firmware)
```

Outcome:

- Configuration backups and firmware upgrades completed in under 2 hours.
- Downtime minimized, with automated verification of the upgrade.

Case Study 2: Building a Custom Monitoring Solution for a Data Center

Scenario

A data center with 200 devices requires a custom monitoring solution to track real-time performance metrics like latency, bandwidth, and device status.

Solution

Python and Dash are used to create a real-time web-based monitoring dashboard.

Implementation:

python

```python
from dash import Dash, dcc, html
from dash.dependencies import Input, Output
import random
import time

# Simulated data for demonstration
devices = [{"id": f"Device-{i}", "ip": f"192.168.0.{i}"} for i in range(1, 201)]

# Simulated metrics function
def fetch_metrics():
    return [
        {"device": d["id"], "latency": random.uniform(1, 100), "status": random.choice(["Online", "Offline"])}
        for d in devices
    ]

app = Dash(__name__)

app.layout = html.Div([
    html.H1("Data Center Monitoring Dashboard"),
    html.Div(id="live-metrics"),
    dcc.Interval(id="interval-component", interval=5000, n_intervals=0)
])

@app.callback(
    Output("live-metrics", "children"),
    [Input("interval-component", "n_intervals")]
```

```
)
def update_metrics(n):
    metrics = fetch_metrics()
    return [
        html.Div([
            html.P(f"Device: {m['device']}"),
            html.P(f"Latency: {m['latency']} ms"),
            html.P(f"Status: {m['status']}")
        ]) for m in metrics
    ]


if __name__ == "__main__":
    app.run_server(debug=True)
```

Outcome:

- Custom dashboard provides real-time visibility into data center performance.
- Metrics help identify issues proactively, reducing downtime.

Case Study 3: Migrating from Manual Processes to Full Network Automation

Scenario

A mid-sized enterprise relies on manual processes for routine tasks like device configuration, VLAN assignments, and ACL management. The goal is to transition to full network automation.

Solution

Python scripts and libraries like Netmiko, NAPALM, and Ansible are used to automate workflows.

Implementation:

- **Task 1: Automate VLAN Assignments**:

    python

    ```
    def configure_vlan(device, vlan_id, vlan_name):
        connection = ConnectHandler(**device)
        commands = [f"vlan {vlan_id}", f"name {vlan_name}"]
        connection.send_config_set(commands)
        connection.disconnect()
    ```

- **Task 2: Automate ACL Management**:

    python

    ```
    def configure_acl(device, acl_name, rules):
        connection = ConnectHandler(**device)
        commands = [f"ip access-list extended {acl_name}"] + rules
        connection.send_config_set(commands)
        connection.disconnect()
    ```

- **Task 3: Integrate Scripts into an Orchestration Tool**: Use Ansible playbooks to trigger Python scripts for large-scale deployments.

Outcome:

- Task completion time reduced by 80%.
- Human errors minimized through automation.
- Improved network consistency and reliability.

---

4. Lessons Learned

Key Takeaways from Case Studies

1. **Automation Reduces Downtime**:
   - Streamlined processes allow faster deployment and recovery.
2. **Custom Solutions Add Value**:
   - Tailored dashboards and workflows provide insights and efficiency.
3. **Scalability Matters**:
   - Scripts must handle growing networks without performance degradation.
4. **Training and Adoption**:

    o Teams need training to effectively manage automated workflows.

These case studies demonstrate the power of Python in solving real-world network challenges, from upgrading devices to monitoring performance and migrating to full automation. By implementing these techniques, organizations can achieve greater efficiency, scalability, and reliability in their network operations.

This concludes the book, ***Python for Network Engineers: Master Python to Automate Networking Tasks and Enhance Network Operations***. You are now equipped with the skills and knowledge to tackle a wide range of networking challenges with Python.

Conclusion and Next Steps

As we reach the conclusion of ***Python for Network Engineers: Master Python to Automate Networking Tasks and Enhance Network Operations***, it's important to reflect on the journey and the wealth of knowledge gained. This book has provided you with a strong foundation in Python-based network automation, empowering you to tackle real-world challenges and improve operational efficiency.

Summary of Key Concepts Learned

1. **Python Fundamentals for Networking**:
   - Mastered Python basics like variables, loops, and file handling.
   - Explored libraries such as **Netmiko**, **NAPALM**, and **Paramiko** to interact with network devices.

2. **Network Automation Techniques**:
   - Automated common tasks like configuration backups, device monitoring, and VLAN management.
   - Unified workflows for multi-vendor environments using Python scripts and APIs.

3. **Advanced Topics**:
   - Implemented **Zero-Touch Provisioning (ZTP)** for device onboarding.
   - Leveraged Python for SDN and NFV integration, enhancing network flexibility and scalability.
   - Built real-time dashboards for monitoring network performance.

4. **Real-World Applications**:

- Studied case studies to understand Python's role in network upgrades, monitoring, and automation migrations.
- Developed solutions for challenges in enterprise, data center, and multi-vendor environments.

Additional Resources for Python and Network Engineering

Python Libraries and Frameworks

1. **Netmiko**: CLI-based automation for multi-vendor devices.
   - GitHub Repository
2. **NAPALM**: Simplifies configuration management across vendors.
   - Official Documentation
3. **PyEZ**: Automate Juniper devices using NETCONF.
   - Juniper PyEZ Documentation
4. **Dash and Flask**: Build interactive dashboards and web applications.
   - Dash Documentation
   - Flask Documentation

Books and Online Courses

1. **Books**:
    - o ***Automate the Boring Stuff with Python*** by Al Sweigart: Perfect for Python beginners.
    - o ***Mastering Python Networking*** by Eric Chou: A deep dive into Python for networking.
2. **Online Courses**:
    - o Cisco DevNet Learning Tracks: Training for network automation.
    - o Coursera - Python for Everybody: Comprehensive Python courses.

Communities and Forums

1. **Reddit**:
    - o r/networking: Discussions on networking challenges and solutions.
2. **GitHub**:
    - o Explore open-source repositories for Python network automation.
3. **Slack and Discord Communities**:
    - o Join networking groups focused on automation and Python scripting.

Encouragement for Continued Learning and Application

1. Experiment and Innovate

- Use the examples in this book as a starting point for your own projects.
- Create scripts that address unique challenges in your network environment.

2. Stay Current

- Follow developments in Python libraries, network technologies, and automation tools.
- Experiment with emerging trends like **Intent-Based Networking (IBN)** and **Artificial Intelligence for IT Operations (AIOps)**.

3. Share Your Knowledge

- Contribute to open-source projects or publish your scripts on platforms like GitHub.
- Join communities to collaborate, learn, and inspire others.

4. Keep Building

- Develop custom tools, dashboards, and workflows to simplify your day-to-day network tasks.

- Pursue certifications like Cisco DevNet or Juniper Automation to enhance your credentials.

Final Thoughts

This book was designed to not only teach you Python for network automation but to inspire confidence in applying these skills to real-world scenarios. As networking evolves, automation will remain at its core, making Python an invaluable tool in your arsenal.

Your journey doesn't end here—it's just the beginning. With every script you write and every network you automate, you're contributing to a smarter, more efficient future in network engineering.

Happy coding and automating! 🚀

www.ingramcontent.com/pod-product-compliance
Lightning Source LLC
LaVergne TN
LVHW052128070326
832902LV00039B/4126